A Breath

A Breath of Fresh Air

from mountain, moor and meadow

Thelma H. Jenkins

Philippian Publications

Philippian Publications
Camden Ridge
Chislehurst, Kent BR7 5EE

Published 1997
Reprinted 2000
ISBN 0 9529314 0 0

Printed in Wales by Creative Print and Design Limited.
Distributed by Bryntirion Press, Bridgend, Glamorgan, South Wales, CF31 4DX.

TO JOHN
MY DEAR HUSBAND
— CALLED TO GLORY 7TH OCTOBER 1996 —
WITH WHOM I SHARED BOTH A DEEP LOVE FOR
WALES, HIS BEAUTIFUL HOMELAND, AND THE FAITH
EXPRESSED IN THESE PAGES.

PHOTOGRAPHS

Contents

Preface

Climbing mountains, walking across the moor or wandering by waterfalls—always there has been a continual longing in my heart to share the beauty all around me with tired workers in busy towns, or weary patients in sick-room or hospital.

Even more, I have longed to share what that beauty reveals of the power and majesty of God, as it has come into my mind in the form of various parables. A short parable can embody profound truth, as we know well from the teaching of our Lord Himself and there are times when, from weariness or even disinclination, we feel able only to read something very simple. When we are sick or over-tired, it grieves us to find our minds sliding wearily over well-loved Bible verses, unable to draw out the richness that we know they contain. Like a sick body, the mind also, at times, needs a light and easily absorbed diet.

The great prophet Moses began his farewell message to the Israelites with these beautiful words: **My doctrine shall drop as the rain, my speech shall distil as the dew, as the small rain upon the tender herb, and as the showers upon the grass:** *Deuteronomy 32:2*

How often, also, have the words of the psalmist been in my heart and upon my lips—**O magnify the Lord with me**—but what does this mean? We cannot make God greater than He is. No, but we can bring His works into nearer focus so that what He really is, or does, becomes clearer to our little human minds, which are often totally unaware of the great miracles of 'nature' surrounding us every moment of our lives.

One autumn, whilst on holiday in Scotland, I glanced through the window at a slender silver birch tree, covered with golden leaves. It was so lovely that I focused my binoculars on it, thus bringing it very much nearer. I then saw that it was shimmering with a thousand rain-drops, every one a pearl glistening in the early morning sunshine. The tree had not changed in any way but, being 'magnified' and brought closer, beauty had been revealed to me that I could not see from a distance.

By bringing some of the works of God's fingers into clearer or nearer focus, it is hoped that this book (which has been distilling through my mind for many years) may lead to a greater depth of wonder and worship; especially, that it may come to all who need it as *A breath of fresh air*.

O magnify the LORD with me, and let us exalt his name together. *Psalm 34:3*

'Nature is not a completed work of art which, outside of God and without Him, exists by itself; but it is God Himself who shows you every night His starry heavens; and every day, His majesty in the colours of the light, in the wonders of the plant and animal world, in the glory of the sea, in the roar of the hurricane, even causing you to hear it sometimes in the rolling of His thunder.

'All nature is nothing else than a living throbbing veil, behind which God hides Himself, and yet in whose folds and undulations He reveals Himself to you, clothed with Majesty.... Through this veil....you must *see* your God in His Almightiness and Divinity.... It is He Who, in all this....lets the fingers of His Majesty work before your eye.

'It is God who causes the lark to sing for you. It is God who cleaves the sea so that its waters foam. It is God who calls the sun from his tent, and at eventide directs his return thereto. It is God who, every evening, lights the twinkling fires in the stars. It is God whose voice rolls down upon you in the thunder.

'And only he who in all this feels the life of God, and in all this clearly sees the Divinity of His Almightiness, understands the glory of the Invisible'.

To be near unto God—Abraham Kuyper

Oh that *men* would praise the LORD *for* his goodness, and *for* his wonderful works to the children of men!

Psalm 107:8

All things praise Thee, Lord, most high,
Heaven and earth, and sea and sky,
All were for Thy glory made,
That Thy greatness, thus displayed,
Should all worship bring to Thee;
All things praise Thee: Lord, may we.

All things praise Thee, night to night
Sings in silent hymns of light;
All things praise Thee, day to day,
Chants Thy power in burning ray;
Time and space are praising Thee:
All things praise Thee: Lord, may we.

All things praise Thee, high and low,
Rain, and dew, and seven-hued bow,
Crimson sunset, fleecy cloud,
Rippling stream, and tempest loud,
Summer, winter, all to Thee
Glory render: Lord, may we.

All things praise Thee: heaven's high shrine
Rings with melody divine;
Lowly bending at Thy feet,
Seraph and archangel meet;
This their highest bliss, to be
Ever praising; Lord, may we.

All things praise Thee—gracious Lord,
Great Creator, powerful Word,
Omnipresent Spirit, now
At Thy feet we humbly bow;
Lift our hearts in praise to Thee:
All things praise Thee: Lord, may we.

(George William Conder)

How we 'accidentally' bought a cottage

Having spent a week in north Wales revelling in the autumn colours we began to travel south, intending to spend the last two or three days of our holiday visiting friends. On the way I was ill and had to spend a day in bed, so we changed our plans and decided to go straight home. As we began our homeward journey, I felt considerably better so we changed our plans yet again, deciding that we would spend our last two days in the south but not visit friends.

On the very last day it rained and rained as it only can rain in Wales—relentless, persisting, drenching rain. We bought some jam doughnuts and drove towards the mountain area, intending to have our coffee and then drive back to our bed and breakfast farm where we knew we would find sanctuary from the weather.

Water was pouring down the lane leading towards the mountains and, with every mile we travelled, it became worse and worse until we seemed to be driving up a stream. I begged my husband to go back (although there was really nowhere that he could turn the car). However, the decision was suddenly made for us when the car spluttered, coughed, jerked, and stopped. So there we were, miles from anywhere, stranded in a car that would not move and with the rain still descending in sheets.

Without realising it, we had stopped right outside a cottage where an elderly gentleman was busy brushing away the flood of water to prevent it from flowing through his garden. He very nobly came to our aid and, after we had turned the car, told us that we would probably be able to 'coast' down to a garage three or four miles away. We were rolling slowly down the road (at about 5 mph) when we realised that there was a car behind us. "Well, we can't go any faster," we said to each other, "it will just have to follow us and be patient." Little did we realise that it was our kind friend, once again coming to our rescue. Knowing that there was a dip in the road which would be our undoing he had followed us in his own car, with a tow-rope, and offered to tow us to a garage.

Were we grateful! We arrived at the garage, still in the teeming rain and, in an effort to thank our benefactor, suggested that he and his wife should have dinner with us in the town that evening. He accepted our invitation and we spent a very pleasant time together. We also presented him with a new tow-rope having managed to snap his during the rescue operation! On parting, our new friends invited us to call on them next time we were in the neighbourhood.

Consequently, next March found us calling at the cottage, having been invited to come for tea. When we walked into the sitting-room and saw the panorama of the mountains from the large patio windows we were almost speechless. During the conversation, our friends told us that they had decided to sell the cottage as it was rather too much for them to manage, and an agent would be coming the very next day to discuss this possibility.

We were actually in the car, on the point of leaving when, for some unknown reason, I said to my husband, "I suppose we could have the details from the agent, couldn't we?" He gave a gulp, as we had no previous intention of buying a cottage and said, "Er—well, yes, I suppose we could." Some seventeen years before we had contemplated buying a cottage because, being born and bred in Cardiff, my husband has always had a hankering to return to his own country. At that time, however, through various circumstances, the Lord had very definitely said, "No!" We asked if our address could be given to the agent and, in less than a week, a letter arrived from our friends, offering us first refusal of the cottage and its contents!

This required much thought and prayer but, having weighed up the remarkable chain of circumstances that had led us to this point, we ultimately decided that it was the Lord's will for us to buy the cottage.

It is strange to think that we had driven up and down that lane for many, many years and had only vaguely realised that there was a cottage there at all. Certainly we would never have imagined that one day we should own it and live there. It is our continual prayer that God will work in us **both to will and to do of *his* good pleasure** (*Philippians 2:13*) and there is no doubt that He willed that I should make what seemed a 'chance' suggestion. How much hinged on that one sentence. What a tremendous difference it has made to our own lives and to the lives of many others. How wonderful it is to know that, in all the apparently haphazard situations of life, God is unceasingly working all things according to the counsel and purpose of His own will.

What a strange chain of providence had led us to this cottage.

If....I had not been ill, we would not have been driving up the lane; we would have been visiting friends instead.

If....I had not felt better we would have returned home two days earlier.

If....it had not been pouring with rain the car would not have broken down outside the cottage; we would not have met the owners nor been invited to visit in the spring.

If....we had not called the very day before the agent was coming to view the cottage we would have known nothing about its possible sale.

If...I had not been strangely prompted to make my chance remark the cottage would never have been offered to us. How much is hidden in that tiny word 'If'!

God moves in a mysterious way
His wonders to perform;
He plants His footsteps in the sea,
And rides upon the storm.

Deep in unfathomable mines
Of never-failing skill,
He treasures up His bright designs,
And works His sovereign will.

Ye fearful saints, fresh courage take,
The clouds ye so much dread
Are big with mercy, and shall break
In blessings on your head.

Judge not the Lord by feeble sense,
But trust Him for His grace;
Behind a frowning providence
He hides a smiling face.

His purposes will ripen fast,
Unfolding every hour;
The bud may have a bitter taste,
But sweet will be the flower.

Blind unbelief is sure to err,
And scan His work in vain;
God is His own interpreter,
And He will make it plain.
(William Cowper)

When darkness veils His lovely face

A visitor from London arrived at the cottage for the first time, late at night, having no idea of her surroundings. Next morning, when she drew back the curtains and saw the sloping fields, the wooded valley and the panorama of the Brecon Beacons stretching to right and left, she could not stop praising the Lord for the beauty and the grandeur spread before her.

The Beacons are not always on display, however. It is possible, in the evening, to sit watching the after-glow of the setting sun turn the mountainside to an unbelievable rose pink; this gradually fades away and the sky above the Beacons becomes deeper and darker as the first stars appear. How extraordinary then, next morning, to look through the window and see—nothing, literally nothing!

A thick grey blanket of cloud reaches to the very doors and windows. Your heart sinks and you think, "This will be a dreadful day" but, within half an hour perhaps, a sudden gleam of light pierces the gloom and an arctic-looking sun shows a pale, anaemic face. Pale it may be but it has power over the blanket of cloud which slowly begins to recede. First the nearby green fields and hedges appear, then the line of trees in the middle distance which always look as though they are marching steadily down to the valley below. The sun gains in power and, as it rises, seems to draw the cloud up with it, gradually revealing the fields, the sheep and the bracken on the further side of the valley. The foothills of the mountains, then the waterfall, come into view until at last almost all the cloud has gone, replaced by brilliant blue sky and a no longer pale but golden sun. The cloud may linger for some time upon the actual peaks, giving the range of mountains the appearance of a smoking volcano, but at long last even that cloud has to give way and there are the mountains—majestic, immovable and undisturbed either by wind or rain, cloud or sun.

There are days when we awake, immersed spiritually in a cloud. This may be caused by sickness, or over-tiredness, (or it may be a direct attack of Satan) but everything seems dark and gloomy and God seems to be remote—a million miles away—if He is there at all. We feel shrouded in gloom and doubt and the only thing that will pierce that dark cloud is faith, however pale and cold it may seem at first.

We never doubted that the mountains were still there in spite of the blanket of thick cloud that blotted them from view. If anyone had suggested that there really were no mountains; that we had only imagined them, we would have answered, "But there *are* mountains, a whole range of them. We have seen them with our own eyes; we have walked on their lower slopes, we have even climbed their peaks. We know they are there."

In the same way our faith has to take deliberate hold of what we have experienced and known of God. We may have to talk to ourselves in these times of darkness as David the psalmist talked to himself when he was depressed and discouraged:

And David was greatly distressed;.... but David encouraged himself in the LORD his God. *1 Samuel 30:6*

Why art thou cast down, O my soul? and *why* art thou disquieted in me? hope thou in God: *for* I shall yet praise him for the help of his countenance. *Psalm 42:5*

We may have to say to ourselves, "I know God is there. I have talked with Him and He has talked with me. I have proved the power of His Word. I have stood firmly on His promises and felt them solid beneath my feet. **God is there** whether I can feel Him or not."

My hope is built on nothing less
Than Jesus' blood and righteousness;
I dare not trust the sweetest frame,
But wholly lean on Jesus' Name.

When darkness veils His lovely face,
I rest on His unchanging grace;
In every high and stormy gale,
My anchor holds within the veil.

On Christ, the solid Rock, I stand;
All other ground is sinking sand.
(Edward Mote)

Declaring our faith in this way will often help to disperse the cloud upon our souls and, although it may be some long time before the 'peaks' appear again, we can steady and comfort ourselves with the truths upon which our faith in God is based and upon our past experience of His blessings. Our feelings may let us down badly but, like the mountains, **God is always there**—majestic, immovable and unchangeable.

LORD, thou hast been our dwelling-place in all generations. Before the mountains were brought forth, or

ever thou hadst formed the earth and the world, even from everlasting to everlasting, thou *art* God.

Psalm 90 :1-2

O God, the Rock of Ages,
Who evermore hast been,
What time the tempest rages,
Our dwelling-place serene:
Before Thy first creations,
O Lord, the same as now;
To endless generations
The Everlasting Thou!

Our years are like the shadows
On sunny hills that lie,
Or grasses in the meadows
That blossom but to die:
A sleep, a dream, a story
By strangers quickly told,
An unremaining glory
Of things that soon are old.

O Thou, Who canst not slumber,
Whose light grows never pale,
Teach us aright to number
Our years before they fail
On us Thy mercy lighten,
On us Thy goodness rest,
And let Thy Spirit brighten,
The hearts Thyself hast blest.

(E.H.Bickersteth)

The heavens declare the glory of God

Sunrise—first of all the faintest line of light behind the distant grey hills, gradually brightening until the sky is a delicate pearl pink, which deepens into varying shades of amber and crimson as the sun emerges from behind a bank of clouds to stream forth in rays of golden light.

Sunset—sometimes a blaze of flaming red and burning gold, set in seas of fiery clouds; sometimes a delicacy of silver and blue, with massed banks of dove-grey clouds hiding the sun from view and, here and there, a break that reveals the blue of deep heaven beyond. Only a thin brush-line of red on the distant horizon indicates the glory of the sun that is setting behind all the cloud. As the sky grows paler and paler, the silver melting into the deep grey and blue, the mountains are already in semi-darkness, topped with billowing white clouds, while the higher strata of fluffy, broken clouds have turned a deep rose pink as they reflect the after-glow of the unseen sunset. Whatever form it takes the sun, rising or setting, is forever confirming the words of the Bible:

The heavens declare the glory of God; and the firmament sheweth his handywork. Day unto day uttereth speech, and night unto night sheweth knowledge.

Psalm 19:1-2

Sunset follows sunrise, sunrise follows sunset. Day after day, year after year yes, century after century, on the vast canvas of the heavens God daily and hourly reveals His glory. One could try to describe a thousand sunsets or sunrises and no two of them would be the same. The God Who makes every tiny snowflake to differ from each other also makes every sunrise and every sunset to differ. How few are the eyes that behold His glory; how many are the eyes that are fastened on the television while these glories are spread above their heads, unheeded and unnoticed.

The spacious firmament on high,
With all the blue ethereal sky,
And spangled heavens, a shining frame,
Their great Original proclaim.
The unwearied sun, from day to day
Does his Creator's power display,
And publishes to every land
The work of an Almighty hand.

Moonlight—the night skies also have their part to play in declaring the glory of their Creator. The delicate wisp of the new crescent moon with the first glowing star low in the evening sky; the radiant and serene light of the full moon remote, majestic, unearthly; the vast galaxies of the stars which God created at the beginning—all still shine down upon our sad and sinful world.

Soon as the evening shades prevail
The moon takes up the wondrous tale,
And nightly to the listen'ing earth
Repeats the story of her birth;
While all the stars that round her burn,
And all the planets in their turn,
Confirm the tidings as they roll,
And spread the truth from pole to pole.

(Joseph Addison)

To town-dwellers, it is a wonderful experience to go into the 'deep' country; to stand in the darkness of a lonely country lane gazing up and up and up into the navy-blue velvet sky at the myriads of stars, knowing that for every star that can be seen there are yet thousands that are invisible. It is thrilling to pick out the seven stars of Orion, still shining forth in perfect formation, just as they did when God spoke words of comfort and hope to his suffering servant Job, thousands of years ago.

His every word of grace is strong
As that which built the skies;
The voice that rolls the stars along
Speaks all the promises.
(Isaac Watts)

Not only do the heavens declare God's glory by their beauty but also, in their never-failing, faultless precision, they confirm His Word, His unchanging decree from the creation of the world. How amazing it is to know that the moon, revolving ceaselessly some 239,000 miles away from the earth, controls the mighty waters of the oceans with such mathematical precision that the tide, in any given place, can be calculated to the very minute for one year or many years ahead!

While the earth remaineth, seed time and harvest, and cold and heat, and summer and winter, and day and night shall not cease. *Genesis 8:22*

The glorious rainbow, seldom seen and then only for a moment or two, glowing against the heavy purple-black rain clouds, declares both the glory and the promise. The luminous colours merging one into the other give a fleeting glimpse of the glory of the God Who covers Himself with light as with a garment. The prophet Ezekiel, recounting his heavenly vision, described the glory that surrounded the throne of God, **As the appearance of the bow that is in the cloud in the day of rain.** In the book of Revelation the apostle John confirmed that he, too, saw **a rainbow round about the throne**. The rainbow is a continuing reminder of God's promise to Noah that never again would He destroy the earth by water.

The full arch of the rainbow, glowing against the thunder clouds, is a magnificent, awe-inspiring sight, but I once saw what one might call the 'broken end' of the rainbow. There had been very heavy early-morning cloud and, as I sat by the edge of a little pool, I noticed that every blade of grass was bearing the tiniest droplet of water. Most of them were just white but here and there, where the sun broke the light, the droplets were red, orange, yellow, blue and green! It was fascinating to pick out the various colours, but I could not see violet, and wondered why. After a few moments, I changed my position, sitting with my back to the sun simply because I was feeling cold. But, of course,'your back to the sun' is the accepted position for seeing rainbows. Now I could see hundreds of these minute, coloured jewels—flaming red, burning orange, glowing yellow, shimmering green, sparkling blue and the most beautiful glistening violet! I gazed and gazed with wonder, for these tiny jewels were so real that a small child would undoubtedly have tried to pick them up with his fingers. Yet it was only 'broken light'—that is all: only another display of God's glory.

Of course, you don't have to believe that God created them to enjoy either sunrise or sunset, moonlight, starlight or rainbow. Many people who are avowed atheists revel in the 'beauties of nature' as they are pleased to call them.

But if the heavens are *not* declaring the glory of God, it all seems rather pointless. What does anyone gain by watching a hundred glorious sunsets? They cannot remember the detail of even one of them, they can only enjoy it while it lasts (probably twenty or thirty minutes at the most) then all that remains is a memory. But if, as we gaze at the glory in the heavens, our hearts are lifted to God in wondering praise and adoration, then we have given to those fleeting moments an eternal quality.

If Thy works praise Thee, Giver of good,
If the sun shines his praise unto Thee,
If the wind, as it sighs thro' the wood,
Makes a murmur of song from each tree,

Then these lips, sure, a tribute shall bring,
Though unworthy the praises must be;
Shall all nature be vocal and sing,
And no psalm of rejoicing from me?
(S.T.Francis)

If, as we enjoy God's glory and power revealed in the heavens, we can give back just a little of the reverent worship that is due to His holy Name, then those moments have become eternal. They will never be lost, either to us or to God Himself, for the praise of His children is exceedingly precious to Him. Oh that we were more like that saint who wondered, all day and every day, at the wisdom of God and the beauty of the world!

By him therefore let us offer the sacrifice of praise to God continually, that is, the fruit of *our* lips giving thanks to his name. *Hebrews 13:15*

O Lord my God, I stand and gaze in wonder
On the vast heavens Thy wisdom hath ordained;
Sun, moon and stars continue at Thy pleasure,
From nothing called and by Thy power sustained.

Sometimes I hear the heavens rent by thunder,
Or see dread lightning leap across the sky,
Then in the cloud I see the promised rainbow
Stilling my fears with mercy from on high.

Nailed to a tree, the great Creator suffered.
When that dread weight of foulest sin He bare.
Lo! Satan flees! the Lord of glory triumphs!
Nothing can with this mighty love compare.

O mighty God, my heart cries out to Thee,
How great Thou art! how great Thou art!
Thy praise shall sound throughout eternity,
How great Thou art! How great Thou art!
(Translated by Eluned Harrison)

The miracle of an egg

One hot summer day, a swallow flew in through the open door and I found it fluttering, in terror and despair, against the window. Swallows are always so endlessly on the move, here one second and gone the next, that there is never time to look at them properly. So, just for a moment, I took the opportunity to study this elusive bird, with its brilliant blue and white colouring and the chestnut feathers round the neck. I had never even realised that there was a row of white spots on the tail feathers but, as the bird hung against the window, his tail was spread out like a fan, making the white spots look like a necklace. I carefully caught the swallow in my hands and set it free to skim away into the blue, such a relieved and happy bird.

Only a few weeks before, that swallow had made a journey of around ten thousand miles from the Sahara desert, in order to build its nest and rear its young in Wales. Ten thousand miles! A frail little bundle of feathers that, in a few weeks, would make that incredible journey back again to its winter quarters with no guide, no compass, no map, yet able to adjust its course by the position of the sun or, when flying at night, by the position of the stars. Some birds (such as cuckoos) migrate to distant lands leaving their young, hatched in this country, to follow them several weeks later, *never having been shown the way and with no older bird to guide them!* Not only has God built into His birds this ability to migrate, but they also know that they must feed more actively before migration, in order to build up the fat reserves they will need for their marathon journeys. The tiny sedge-warbler, weighing ¾ oz (less than a tablespoonful of sugar) can double its weight giving it enough fuel to fly, without rest, for between 60 and 90 hours as it journeys to the south of the Sahara. One would think that the wonder of migration would qualify for being classed as a miracle? Yet people pass it off by saying, "Yes, isn't nature wonderful?" "Nature?" remarked a man of God, "What is nature but God at work in His own world?"

For the grandeur of Thy nature,
Grand beyond a seraph's thought;
For created works of power,
Works with skill and kindness wrought;
For Thy providence, that governs
Through Thine empire's wide domain,
Wings an angel, guides a sparrow;
Blessèd be Thy gentle reign.
(Robert Robinson)

On a breezy autumn afternoon, I walked along the sheep path between banks of russet and gold bracken and thought of the birds I had watched and heard in the previous months. There had been the wheatears and their three fluffy babies flitting along the dry-stone wall which contained their nest; the cuckoo calling from the wood; the flock of young swallows flying restlessly to and from a gnarled grey hawthorn, obviously practising for the great 'take-off' day that was approaching. Where were they now? Incredibly, they were thousands of miles away in West or Central Africa! Yet, more incredible still, I knew that 'sure as clock-work' they would be back again in March or April.

In the early days of March I walked along the same path, but there were no wheatears. A few days later and, sure enough, there they were, bobbing about on the same piece of wall where their nest had been the previous year. Those tiny birds had once again made their amazing journey of several thousand miles arriving back in the right place, at the right time guided, not by 'clock-work', but by the amazing instinct which God, their Creator, has built into His tiny birds, His little feathered computers!

The works of the LORD *are* great, sought out of all them that have pleasure therein....He hath made his wonderful works to be remembered: *Psalm 111:2* and *4*

We do not marvel because we think we know it all. Suppose, for a moment, that you did **not** know where birds came from. If someone showed you the slimy contents of an egg and showed you a little bird—bones and feathers, beak and claws and tiny, bright little eyes—and they said to you, "This egg will turn into that," you would never believe them. You would say, "Impossible! Nothing short of a miracle could turn that egg into a flying, singing bird." That is quite true. It *is* nothing short of a miracle; a miracle that happens millions of times, every spring and summer in every country of the world. Yet we just say, "Oh yes; everybody knows that birds come from eggs. There's nothing new in that." No, there is nothing new in it, but there is everything in it for wonder and amazement and worship.

Oh that *men* would praise the LORD *for* his goodness, and *for* his wonderful works to the children of men!

Psalm 107:8

Think again of the last time you looked at the contents of an egg. Think again of the last time you saw a skylark mounting up to heaven on its tiny wings and heard it pouring forth an endless cascade of silvery notes. It has been said that if all the notes that a skylark sings in one day were to be written down as music, it would take a composer such as Beethoven all his life to write them into symphonies. All that music, stored in the little crested head of a skylark and poured forth from his tiny throat; yet, only a few months before, he was merely the unattractive contents of an egg! Miracles still happen and a 'miracle' happens every time a bird is hatched. Surely the hymn of our childhood says it all:

Each little flower that opens,
Each little bird that sings,
He made their glowing colours,
He made their tiny wings:

He gave us eyes to see them,
And lips that we might tell
How great is God Almighty,
Who has made all things well:

All things bright and beautiful,
All creatures great and small,
All things wise and wonderful,
The Lord God made them all.

(Cecil Frances Alexander)

N.B. The word 'miracle' (here and elsewhere) is used in its second dictionary definition:"a remarkable event or object"—*Oxford Dictionary.*

A consuming fire

An old-fashioned log fire with pine logs, pine cones and branches from the fig tree sending out a strange, sweet fragrance as they burn is one of the delights of Christmas. Fire is a comfort and a pleasure when it is safely controlled and, with very careful supervision, it can even become a plaything! Two young relatives, visiting us at Christmas and accustomed only to electric fires, were entranced when they were allowed, with grown-ups watching, to throw balls of used wrapping paper into the fire, especially the paper that produced weird flickering flames of pink or mauve or green.

Some months later, in the hot mid-summer, I was lying in bed reading. It was close on midnight and the windows were wide open in the hope of catching the least stray breath of cool air. I heard a sound which puzzled me, because I could not register what it was. Three times I went to the window, wondering why I could hear water pouring on a gravel surface. The third time, however, I smelt a 'bonfire' smell and realised, with horror, that flames were leaping up beyond the trees that screened the golf-course. The mysterious sound was not water pouring upon gravel, but the intermittent crackling of burning undergrowth and grass!

Immediately, I dialled 999 to report the fire, quite expecting to be told that the Fire Brigade had already received half-a-dozen telephone calls, but this was not the case. Indeed, twenty minutes later, as I was still watching the flames leaping higher and higher, I received a call saying, "We can't find the fire!" I could hardly believe my ears and tried to give more explicit directions although it was difficult, from that distance, to describe the actual location of the fire. What a relief it was, a short while later, to hear the heavy throb of a fire-engine, the high-pitched whine of water being pumped from a hydrant and men's voices directing operations. Driving past next day, I quite expected to see a large expanse of blackened golf-course but there was no sign of there having been a fire. Evidently it was well inside the heart of the wood, some distance from the road, and that was why it had been hard to locate.

'Fire is a good servant but a terrible master'. When we are in a position to control the fire and make it serve our need, even our pleasure, it seems harmless enough but a fire that is out of control is probably the most fearful sight on earth.

The Bible describes God as a 'consuming fire'. This is a terrible picture but it is probably the only way that we can begin to understand anything of His burning holiness. The holiness of God is like a white-hot fire that consumes all that is evil and unclean and unholy. This truth was once brought home to me very vividly. I found a vole in my kitchen and a vole is an attractive little mouse creature—but not this one! It had been brought in by one of the cats and, having escaped, had subsequently died behind a cupboard. By the time I found it, although it was dead, in another sense it was very much 'alive'! Hastily I averted my eyes and, grabbing an old newspaper, hurried with it to the bonfire. I was glad that there was such a thing as a consuming fire to burn up something so corrupt and repulsive.

Art thou not from everlasting, O LORD my God, mine Holy One?.... Thou art of purer eyes than to behold evil, and canst not look on iniquity. *Habakkuk 1:12-13*

The very holiness of God's nature constitutes Him our enemy, but if this is so, how can we ever hope to draw near to Him? It is no more possible for us, as sinners, to approach the High and Holy God and not be consumed, than it is possible for dry leaves and bracken to resist an approaching fire.

....let us have grace, whereby we may serve God acceptably with reverence and godly fear: For our God *is* a consuming fire. *Hebrews 12:28-29*

A consuming fire. This is a solemn thought for the Christian. He has to search his life to see whether he is producing lasting things such as gold, silver and precious stones that can pass, unscathed, through the testing of God's fire, or whether he is only producing rubbish—wood, hay and stubble—that will all be burnt up by God's holy judgment.

For other foundation can no man lay than that is laid, which is Jesus Christ. Now if any man build upon this foundation gold, silver, precious stones, wood, hay, stubble; Every man's work shall be made manifest: for the day shall declare it, because it shall be revealed by fire; and the fire shall try every man's work of what sort it is.

1 Corinthians 3:11-13

A consuming fire. This is even more solemn for the non-Christian for he, too, will be called to stand before the judgment seat of God. If he has rejected Christ as his Saviour, he will have nothing to protect him from God's holy and eternal wrath against his sin, for the Bible says: **Who shall be punished with everlasting destruction from the presence of the Lord, and from the glory of his power;**

2 Thessalonians 1:9

Eternal Light! Eternal Light!
How pure the soul must be,
When, placed within Thy searching sight,
It shrinks not, but with calm delight
Can live and look on Thee.

The spirits that surround Thy throne
May bear the burning bliss;
But that is surely theirs alone,
Since they have never, never known
A fallen world like this.

O how shall I, whose native sphere
Is dark, whose mind is dim,
Before the Ineffable appear,
And on my naked spirit bear
The uncreated beam?

There is a way for man to rise
To that sublime abode:
An offering and a sacrifice,
A Holy Spirit's energies,
An Advocate with God.

These, these prepare us for the sight
Of holiness above;
The sons of ignorance and night
Can dwell in the eternal Light
Through the eternal Love. *(Thomas Binney)*

When God says, "No!"

A pair of coal tits, little buff coloured birds with black and white heads, had decided to nest in the rockery. They made endless journeys across the lawn, always alighting on a swaying branch of the white cherry tree to take a good look round, before they swooped into a narrow opening leading to a hidden, cosy hole inside the stone wall. What could be better? I watched with great interest as the busy little birds flew in and out, building their nest; but both the birds and I had forgotten the cats, Tinker and Topsy. They also found it very interesting when the parent birds began to fly endlessly in and out with food for their nestlings!

Oh! the trouble I had trying to protect my birds. I made a barricade of holly thinking that would surely deter any animal, only to find that Topsy, the fluffy cat, had jumped right into the middle and was standing with her nose by the opening in the rock. More than one spring morning, being wakened about five o'clock by the birds' dawn chorus, I looked out of the window and then ran hastily into the garden to turn on the sprinkler. This seemed to be the only certain method of keeping the cats away. The coal tits and the cats must have wondered why it was always raining in that part of the garden! At last, the baby birds were safely fledged, but I vowed to myself, "Never again".

Next spring, I filled up all the holes in the wall with large stones, or tufts of pine needles dropped by the squirrels. The coal tits perched on the swaying branch of the white cherry tree, as before, peering into their previous home and obviously wondering why they could not get in there again. It was

such an ideal place and I could almost feel their frustration and disappointment. It would have required no effort on my part to walk down the garden, remove the stones or pine-tufts and let them have what they wanted, yet nothing would induce me to do this. Why? Because I could not be bothered? Because I was hard-hearted and did not care? No, quite the reverse. It was because, with a wiser intelligence than they possessed and a foresight of what would happen, I knew the troubles that would be theirs if they succeeded in nesting there again. I knew the potential danger of the cats, which they had presumably forgotten. I knew the distress and anxiety that would be theirs when the eggs were hatched and, because I cared, I would not let them have their desire.

This hardly needs any application. Can we not see ourselves, in those two little birds, so intent upon the ideal thing (or so we think). "It must be God's will for us; it is so perfect; it is just what we need." Yet God says, "No!" In His infinite wisdom and knowledge He is aware of dangers and sorrows which we could never foresee.

No one would question that my action was right with respect to the coal tits, although it appeared to be very unkind; yet I am only mortal, and they were only birds. But God is the all-wise, the all-loving Creator and we are the creatures that He dearly loves. What is more, He really does know what is best, not only for our physical lives but, more important still, what is wisest and best for our spiritual and eternal well-being. He knows, also, the plans that He has in mind for our future work in His Kingdom. That is why sometimes (although not always, by any means) God has to say "No!"

Choose for us, God, nor let our weak preferring
Cheat our poor souls of good Thou hast designed;
Choose for us, God, Thy wisdom is unerring,
And we are fools and blind.

Sometimes we learn, through later events, why God said, "No!" Sometimes we discover, to our joy, that the answer must have been "Yes—but not yet!" Sometimes we never know why, we just have to trust His love and wisdom, knowing that He is: 'Too wise to be mistaken, too good to be unkind.'

He knows; He loves; He cares;
Nothing this truth can dim;
He gives the very best to those
Who leave the choice with Him.
(Author unknown)

When Amy Carmichael (one of God's faithful missionary servants) was only a little girl of three years old, she longed to have beautiful blue eyes like her mother. Having been taught that God always hears and answers prayer she asked one night, in her bed-time prayers, that God would change her brown eyes into blue eyes. Confidently and eagerly next morning she climbed on a chair to look in the mirror at her blue eyes. To her amazement they were still brown. God had not answered her prayer! How could that be? Years later, even as an adult, she could remember her bewilderment and disappointment and the words that came into her baby mind from somewhere (perhaps from her mother) "Isn't 'No' an answer?" That was a hard lesson for a child. It is an equally hard lesson for an adult.

Only a child, of course, would ask for the colour of her eyes to be changed, not realising that the Lord had already made them the colour He intended. Many years later, when Amy was working among Indian women, it was necessary for her to mingle with them in native costume. Only then did she learn why she had been born with brown eyes instead of blue. Indian women always have brown eyes and, however correct her clothing, her blue eyes would have betrayed her immediately as a foreigner. God knew, long before she was born, the great work that He had in mind for her to do in India and for that work *it was essential that her eyes should be brown*. **Known unto God are all his works from the beginning of the world**.

Acts 15:18.

Our eyes see dimly till by faith anointed,
And our blind choosing brings us grief and pain;
Through Him alone Who hath our way appointed,
We find our peace again.

Let us press on, in patient self-denial,
Accept the hardship, shrink not from the loss;
Our portion lies beyond the hour of trial,
Our crown beyond the cross.

(W.H.Burleigh)

A friend in need

Snow had fallen during the night but, by mid-morning, the wintery sun was shining and many birds were eagerly searching for food. Walking into the garden, to my delight I saw a redwing, the smallest of our thrushes, sitting on the bank where the pussy-willow and lady's smock grow. I had never seen a redwing in my garden before, but my delight was quickly tempered with sadness for it was evidently a very sick little bird. Crouching on the wet earth, its eyes were partially closed and its body shaken with spasms of trembling. It looked as if it were about to die.

As I approached, it tried to struggle into the bushes and although wanting to help, I knew I was only adding to its misery. There was nothing I could do but take this unusual opportunity of studying it, close at hand, looking at its lovely markings, especially the brilliant red beneath its wings. I worshipped the Lord who had fashioned His creature so beautifully, yet I was sad that my pleasure should come out of the bird's suffering and extremity. It looked so forlorn and I felt sure that it was envying the busy, active birds all around, longing to be one with them, but set apart because of its weakened condition.

Standing there, watching, I suddenly saw what a picture this was of our own lives. Usually we are the busy ones, active in the Lord's work here, there and everywhere, giving hardly a passing thought to His sick and weaker children. Then one day, unexpectedly perhaps, the roles are reversed. We are the sick, the weak, the ailing, no longer able to join in the things in which we once delighted. We look wistfully at our friends and companions, wishing that we could be active as they are.

But—it was only because the redwing was so weak and inactive that I had that opportunity to study and marvel at the wonderful works of God's fingers and to see, in detail, the beauty of His fashioning. Had that bird been as the others, it would have flashed past me in a second and I could never have studied it so carefully. So it is with ourselves. The people who watch us when we are sick and laid aside should be able (we hope) to see more clearly the marks of God's grace, the fruits of His Spirit, the wonder of His working in our lives: things which may not be seen so clearly when we are busy and active. We also experience a fellow-feeling of pity and sympathy that we may never have known before, for those who are laid aside in weakness; we understand how shut out they feel, how frustrated, how lonely and useless. Words that we have sung, in all sincerity, in our happier days, come back to us with a deeper significance:

More of Thy glory let me see,
Thou Holy, Wise and True!
I would Thy living image be,
In joy and sorrow too.
(Johann Caspar Lavater)

There was a happy ending for my little redwing. Half-an-hour later, looking out of my kitchen window, I saw another redwing fly down to the first one who, seemingly encouraged, made a few struggling hops to reach some melted snow. It took a sip or two and then suddenly flew into the air with the second bird, away over the trees and out of sight. Presumably the first bird was suffering from exhaustion after a long flight and the second bird (was it her mate?) had come back to look for her and encourage her to continue the journey. There's something to be learned from the second redwing, too!

Lord, speak to me, that I may speak
In living echoes of Thy tone;
As Thou hast sought, so let me seek
Thy erring children lost and lone.

O strengthen me, that, while I stand
Firm on the rock, and strong in Thee,
I may stretch out a loving hand
To wrestlers with the troubled sea.

O give Thine own sweet rest to me,
That I may speak with soothing power
A word in season,as from Thee,
To weary ones in needful hour.

O use me, Lord, use even me,
Just as Thou wilt, and when, and where,
Until Thy blessed face I see,
Thy rest, Thy joy, Thy glory share.
(Frances Ridley Havergal)

As in a mirror

Not far from the cottage, just beyond the cattle-grid and on the very edge of the moor, there is a 'part-time' pool. During the hot, dry summer it is only noticeable as a dip in the level of the grassland but in the spring, after the snows have melted and the heavy rains have fallen, it becomes quite an expanse of water, irregular in shape, set in the midst of green grass and russet-coloured bracken.

The pool, in itself, is nothing much to look at. A small child in bright red 'wellies' goes happily splashing through, churning it into a mass of muddy water. Then the child is taken home for tea, the muddy water gradually settles again and, as the sun begins to sink in the western sky, the little pool becomes a mirror reflecting the blue sky high above, the dove-grey clouds and the black silhouette of bare trees on a nearby hill, out-lined against the pinks and mauves of the setting sun. This only happens on a very still evening. The slightest breeze ruffling the surface will shatter the reflection so that nothing is to be seen but the rippling water.

'Shallow and muddy'—words that describe not only the pool but, sadly, the lives that most of us live, especially if we compare them with the beauty and perfection of the life of the Lord Jesus Christ. His life is like a deep and vast reservoir, reflecting mile upon mile of woods and hills, forests and snowcapped mountains or glorious sunlit skies with masses of white billowing clouds. Indeed, there is no comparison at all between His life and ours. Even the lives of the greatest Christians are only shallow and muddy when compared with His. Yet those

who are truly His people are intended, in spite of their shallowness, to reflect something of His glory and holiness, for God is always working to conform us to the image of His Son.

Let the beauty of Jesus be seen in me,
All His wondrous compassion and purity;
O Thou Spirit divine, All my nature refine,
Till the beauty of Jesus be seen in me.

(T.Jones)

When we allow the daily events of life to 'churn us up' as they so often do, we resemble the pool in its muddy condition, and there is no reflection for anyone to see. When we allow the things that other people do and say to 'ruffle us up' then, again, the reflection is broken. Shallow and muddy—yet there are times, in spite of our continual failings and weaknesses, when we are able to reflect just a little of His glory and beauty.

But we all, with open face beholding as in a glass the glory of the Lord, are changed into the same image from glory to glory, even as by the Spirit of the Lord.

2 Corinthians 3:18

Under a brilliant blue sky and despite the biting cold, we stood on a January day beside a vast reservoir, gazing at the reflection in the deep, unmoving waters. It was almost too perfect to be true. Every dip and gully and rock on the snow was faithfully reflected in the water, down to the leafless shrubs and dead bracken at the water's edge, and the icicles dripping from the rocky ledges. We looked up to see if the reflection really tallied with the mountain and, of course, it was correct to the smallest detail, because of the amazing stillness of the water.

On another occasion, I stood by a different reservoir on a

crisp autumn morning and saw such a clear reflection of sky and fields, sheep and farmhouses that it was like looking at an inverted picture almost a mile long! After gazing at it for a while, I drove to the other side of the reservoir but when I returned about fifteen minutes later, the faintest of breezes was stirring the water and the whole picture had been completely shattered.

So the parable unfolds and the principle is always the same for deep reservoir or shallow moorland pool—and for the lives that are intended to show forth the beauty of God in the Lord Jesus Christ—'The stiller the water the clearer the reflection'.

Dear Lord and Father of mankind,
Forgive our foolish ways;
Re-clothe us in our rightful mind;
In purer lives Thy service find,
In deeper reverence, praise.

With that deep hush subduing all
Our words and works that drown
The tender whisper of Thy call,
As noiseless let Thy blessing fall,
As fell Thy manna down.

Drop Thy still dews of quietness,
Till all our strivings cease;
Take from our souls the strain and stress,
And let out ordered lives confess
The beauty of Thy peace.

(J.G.Whittier)

All we like sheep

Drawing back the curtains one morning and looking across into the field on the other side of the road, I noticed a sheep lying under a hedge on the bank, seemingly having spent the night there in great comfort. Two or three hours later my husband called me and said, "There's a sheep in the field and it's caught in a thick bramble and can't get away." Sure enough, it was the sheep I had seen earlier, now standing on her feet, looking very puzzled and obviously wondering why she could not get away from the hedge, presumably having spent the night there by force and not by choice. The bramble was very thick and strong and the more the sheep struggled to free herself, the more tightly it was becoming embedded in her woollen fleece.

The rest of the flock ambled past her, evidently feeling that it was no concern of theirs. One of them stopped for a moment to look at her, as though to say, 'I see you have problems and I wish I could help you, but what can I do? There's just no way that I can set you free!' As we watched, the entangled sheep made another effort to free herself, with no more success than before, then nibbled rather hopelessly at the grass within reach having, no doubt, already eaten all that was any good.

It was evident that we must do something for her so we telephoned the farmer who, after about twenty minutes, came riding up in his Land-Rover, strode into the field and, with a strong pair of cutters, set the sheep free. He watched her go ambling off in search of the rest of the flock, apparently none

the worse for her hours of solitary confinement. Had she been in a hidden corner of the field, she could have been in that condition for several days. Had this happened to a sheep out on the wild mountain side she would probably have starved to death or been attacked, in her helpless condition, by predators.

A few months earlier, we had seen a sheep lying on her back (in a different field this time) and we knew that this was very serious. On this occasion, our telephone call brought the farmer up in next to no time. We heard his Land-Rover tearing down the lane and then saw him running across the field. He quickly heaved the animal on to her feet and watched her for a few minutes. Speaking to us as he drove home again, he said that she would be all right, but in another half-an-hour she would have been dead. Apparently the gases from the partly-consumed grass in her stomach would very soon have caused her to choke. The farmer had lost a sheep only the week before because she had been lying on her back too long and no one had seen her in time to help. The sheep lies down to scratch her back on the grass and then finds that, with the heavy weight of wool she is carrying before shearing, she cannot get to her feet again.

Sheep are silly creatures, so often getting themselves into difficulties and usually quite unable to help themselves. In both these instances, the sheep could not help herself, neither could the other sheep give her any help. It needed a totally different kind of being with different powers to set them free. It is easy to see why humans are often classed as sheep in the Bible.

Know ye that the LORD he *is* God: *it is* he *that* hath made us, and not we ourselves; *we are* his people, and the sheep of his pasture. *Psalm 100:3.*

Humans are both silly and sinful. We also get ourselves into awkward situations and then find we cannot get out of them. Sometimes a person may feel deeply concerned about his sin, knowing himself to be hopelessly entangled, like the sheep caught in the bramble and with no ability at all to set himself free. His friends may be totally indifferent (as most of the sheep were) or, even if they are sympathetic, they have no way of setting anyone else free from the entanglement of sin. In both of the instances referred to the sheep needed her owner, the farmer, to come to her rescue and we need our Owner, God Himself, to come to our rescue. He alone has the power and ability to set us free from the sin that ensnares us.

All we like sheep have gone astray; we have turned every one to his own way; and the LORD hath laid on him the iniquity of us all. *Isaiah 53:6*

If the Son therefore shall make you free, ye shall be free indeed. *John 8 :36*

It is always a delight to see a flock of sheep grazing contentedly on the moor, with the sun shining down on their woolly backs. One of the prettiest sights in spring-time is to see a string of baby lambs, some only a few weeks old, racing round the edge of the field in a pre-bedtime scamper. There is usually one who is the leader and he starts racing from one corner of the field to the other (preferably on a raised bank if there is one) with anything from ten to twenty other lambs following. They will do this over and over again, perhaps to use up their spare energy before settling down for the night—like little children who say, "One more time, Mummy. Just one more game before bed!" It is lovely to hear their little hooves drumming over the grass and to see them suddenly stop and leap off the ground, all four feet at once, as if they were on springs.

The Bible continually uses the picture of the lamb, so innocent and harmless, to describe the Son of God, the Lord of Glory. At the very beginning of His public ministry, the moment John the Baptist saw Him, he cried out for all to hear:
Behold the Lamb of God, which taketh away the sin of the world. *John 1:29*

Our Lord knew that He had been born into the world for the sole purpose of dying in the place of sinners. His death did not take Him by surprise. He knew Himself to be, in very truth, the Lamb of God. He knew the exact time and all the terrible details of His death and spoke of it many times to his disciples.

From that time forth began Jesus to shew unto his disciples, how that he must go unto Jerusalem, and suffer many things of the elders and chief priests and scribes, and be killed, and be raised again the third day.

Matthew 16:21

Strange as it may seem, our Lord was both the Lamb who came to die for sinners *and* the Shepherd who came to seek them. Toward the close of His ministry, as His death drew nearer and nearer, our Lord spoke of Himself as the Good Shepherd.

I am the good shepherd: the good shepherd giveth his life for the sheep.....I lay down my life for the sheep....No man taketh it from me, but I lay it down of myself. I have power to lay it down and I have power to take it again.

John 10 :11,15,18.

There were ninety and nine that safely lay
In the shelter of the fold;
But one was out on the hills away,
Far off from the gates of gold—
Away on the mountains wild and bare,
Away from the tender Shepherd's care.

But none of the ransomed ever knew
How deep were the waters crossed,
Nor how dark was the night that the Lord passed through
Ere He found His sheep that was lost.
Out in the desert He heard its cry,
Sick, and helpless and ready to die.

'Lord, whence are those blood-drops all the way,
That mark out the mountain's track?'
'They were shed for one who had gone astray
Ere the Shepherd could bring him back.'
'Lord, whence are Thy hands so rent and torn?'
'They are pierced to-night with many a thorn.'

But all through the mountains, thunder-riven,
And up from the rocky steep,
There rose a cry to the gate of heaven,
'Rejoice! I have found my sheep!'
And the angels echoed around the throne:
'Rejoice! for the Lord brings back His own!'
(Elizabeth Cecilia Clephane)

New lives for old

Surprise at Christmas! As the red velvet curtains were drawn to shut out the cold and darkness a peacock butterfly, cheated by the warmth of the log-fire into thinking that spring had come already, fluttered into the centre of the room and settled on my finger. While it dithered in its mind, not sure where to go or what to do next, I had a delightful few moments studying the exquisite coloured markings on its wings. Then I carefully carried it to a dark corner of the wood-shed, where it could hide away safely until the March sunshine would draw it out, at the proper time, into the garden.

If it were possible (which presumably it is not) for a caterpillar to watch a butterfly fluttering past in the air on its gossamer wings, there would be no way of convincing that caterpillar that one day it would change into such a brilliant creature; that one day, its ignominious, crawling, earth-bound existence would be ended and it, too, would flutter in the blue sky on jewel-coloured wings, sipping nectar from the flowers.

Yet this is another miracle that is continually taking place. The caterpillar passes into a form of death, a 'sleep' and lies, bound and still within the chrysalis, waiting for the warmth of the spring sunshine. When that touch comes, sure enough, it emerges from its 'tomb' with a new body suited to a totally new and different life.

From a caterpillar—to a chrysalis—to a butterfly! Could there possibly be a better illustration of the change that awaits the Christian in the sleep of death? The Bible tells us that those who die trusting in the Lord Jesus Christ as their Saviour from sin 'fall asleep' in Jesus. They will be raised from that sleep to find themselves possessed of a new and glorious body, just like the glorious body that our Lord had after His death and resurrection; a body no longer subject to pain or disease, to weakness or death. Not only will there be a new body, but a new and sinless life for which that body is fitted, but who is able to speak of that?

Eye hath not seen, nor ear heard, neither have entered into the heart of man, the things which God hath prepared for them that love him. *1 Corinthians 2:9*

My knowledge of that life is small,
The eye of faith is dim;
But 'tis enough that Christ knows all,
And I shall be with Him!
(Richard Baxter)

A friend of mine went into her garden one evening to tidy the flower border. Turning over the moist, dark earth with her fork she saw what appeared to be a tightly coiled wire spring but, as she picked it up, she felt it move in her hand. It was alive! It was not a wire spring but a chrysalis! Placing it carefully on the wooden fence she stood very still, waiting and watching.

She watched the chrysalis quiver once or twice and then, as it split open at the upper end, out came a tiny head, followed by a small, furry body with crumpled, wet wings hanging from its shoulders.

She watched the butterfly cling to the fence with its tiny fragile feet, probing the air with its hair-like antennae while its wings, drying and hardening in the warm spring sunshine, began to expand, taking on colour and many varied markings.

She watched the wings open and close, open and close until, after about half-an-hour, a perfect small tortoiseshell butterfly, complete with 'tortoise-shell' stripes and reddish/amber wings edged with the dark border and lovely pale blue crescents, flew away into the glorious light of the evening sunshine. What an experience! What a privilege!

Behold, I shew you a mystery; We shall not all sleep, but we shall all be changed, In a moment, in the twinkling of an eye, at the last trump: for the trumpet shall sound, and the dead shall be raised incorruptible, and we shall be changed. *1 Corinthians 15:51-52*

Out of my bondage, sorrow and night,
Jesus, I come; Jesus, I come;
Into Thy freedom, gladness and light,
Jesus, I come to Thee.
Out of my sickness into Thy health.
Out of my want and into Thy wealth,
Out of my sin and into Thyself,
Jesus, I come to Thee.

Out of the fear and dread of the tomb,
Jesus, I come; Jesus, I come;
Into the joy and light of Thy home,
Jesus, I come to Thee.
Out of the depths of ruin untold,
Into the peace of Thy sheltering fold,
Ever Thy glorious face to behold,
Jesus, I come to Thee.

(W.T.Sleeper)

The smitten tree

Within ten minutes steady walking from the cottage, there is a small moorland pool, a little jewel set in the green turf, where the sheep and wild horses come to drink. Gorse, willow and crab-apple trees grow in the foreground while the majestic Beacons make an impressive back-drop. Amongst all this beauty there is a dead tree outlined against the very centre of the mountains and one almost feels that it ought not to be there. It seems out of place when everything else is so lovely.

The wild horses do not often visit the pool, but one afternoon I surprised seven of them there. Five were quietly cropping the grass, while the sixth was standing in the water with a yard of pond-weed dangling from his mouth. The seventh was having a nose-to-nose conversation with a horse in the nearby field, obviously telling him how much more exciting it was to be a wild horse, free to roam at will all over the moor, than to be shut in one field all the time.

At this point, two young fillies (dark brown and chestnut in colour) decided to have a frolic. Just as puppies will play together, growling and biting, but only in fun, so these fillies were having a pretend fight. They kept rubbing heads and noses and then whirling round and kicking with their hooves. Then they would rise on their hind legs and pretend to strike with their forefeet. Their blonde manes and tails were all ruffled with the wind and they looked so wild and beautiful. This went on until they found themselves in the edge of the pool, where they continued their frolic, splashing the muddy water up their legs.

I was watching from the other side of the pool through my binoculars and they seemed so close that I almost wondered why I was not getting splashed as well! At last they had a canter round the bank and I stood up rather quickly. I was sheltering from the wind behind a large gorse bush and I did not fancy them finishing their frolic on top of me. However, at this point a lovely creamy coloured horse (probably the leading mare) gave one of the fillies a nip as if to say, "That's enough! That's enough! You're making too much of a disturbance." This quietened them down a little, but all the time the sun was shining out of such a blue sky, the clouds were very high and a skylark was singing his endless song over my head.

One day, approaching the pool from a different angle, I suddenly saw that the dead tree (which I had wished was not there) was rather like a cross; not exactly so, but nearly. It looked stark and bare as though it had once been smitten by lightning. I found myself thinking that it was typical, not only of the Cross, but of the Lord Jesus Christ Himself, for the words kept coming into my mind: **Surely he hath borne our griefs, and carried our sorrows: yet we did esteem him stricken, smitten of God, and afflicted**. *Isaiah 53:4.*

I realised that all the loveliness around me—the golden gorse and the mounting skylarks; the liquid song of the willow warbler and the haunting cry of the curlew; the cuckoo calling in beautiful monotony from the nearby wood; the great mountains in the background with the passing clouds making patches of shade and sunshine—in fact, the endless variation of beauty on every side was only possible for me, and for all men, because He had been smitten and afflicted. He endured all the suffering and anguish, so that we could enjoy all these beautiful works of His fingers. The smitten tree, far from being unwanted in that lovely scene, had suddenly become the centre, the focal point, just as the Cross of the Lord Jesus Christ—cruel, stark and terrible—is the focal point of history and creation. All history leads up to the Cross, all history leads away from the Cross.

In the cross of Christ I glory,
Towering o'er the wrecks of time:
All the light of sacred story
Gathers round its head sublime.

Bane and blessing, pain and pleasure,
By the cross are sanctified;
Peace is there that knows no measure,
Joys that through all time abide.
(John Bowring)

When, through their wilful disobedience, Adam and Eve broke their fellowship with God, He drove them out of the Garden of Eden but not before He had promised that, one day, He would send a Saviour into the world.

Through all the centuries the world waited for this promised Saviour and, when He came, He achieved the 'impossible'—a life of perfect obedience to God. The focal point of all history is not only the Cross, but the spotless life that led up to it. *Without that spotless life there could have been no Cross.* During the thirty-three years that He lived on this earth our Lord never once sinned against God His Father.

For we have not an high priest which cannot be touched with the feeling of our infirmities; but was in all points

tempted like as *we are, yet* without sin. Let us therefore come boldly unto the throne of grace, that we may obtain mercy, and find grace to help in time of need.

Hebrews 4:15-16.

It only required one sin on the part of Adam and Eve to break their fellowship with God. It only required one sin on the part of our Lord to make it impossible for Him to become our Saviour. How do we know that He did not sin when we have no detailed record of His life? Because had He sinned but once, death would have held Him captive. By His triumphant resurrection we know that Satan had no power to hold Him.

And declared *to be* the Son of God with power, according to the spirit of holiness, by the resurrection from the dead. *Romans 1:4*

What grace, O Lord, and beauty shone
Around Thy steps below!
What patient love was seen in all
Thy life and death of woe!

For ever on Thy burdened heart
A weight of sorrow hung,
Yet no ungentle, murmuring word
Escaped Thy silent tongue.

Thy foes might hate, despise, revile,
Thy friends unfaithful prove,
Unwearied in forgiveness still,
Thy heart could only love.

(Edward Denny)

We are unable to live one day without sin. Our Lord lived a sinless life in a small village, amongst petty-minded people like ourselves, not for a day, nor for a week, but for thirty years. Not one angry look, not one impatient word, not one irritable gesture marred His life. God the Father could say of Him:

This is my beloved Son, in whom I am well pleased.

Matthew 3:17

God the Son could truthfully say:

I do always those things that please him.

John 8:29

Those years in obscurity were followed by three years in the full glare of publicity with the adulation of the thronging multitudes, the bickering of His disciples and the spite and hatred of His enemies. Yet, in the midst of it all, He lived His holy, blameless life. Adam sinned in the perfection of the Garden of Eden. Our Lord did not sin even when He was dying in agony upon an instrument of torture. Well might we sing:

Upon a life I did not live,
Upon a death I did not die,
Another's life, Another's death,
I stake my whole eternity.

(Author unknown)

It is a great mystery, deep beyond our understanding, But, thank God, we can understand, in some measure, a 'broken body' and 'poured-out blood'. We can see in them, the offering up of that sinless life on our behalf to God. Here is an atonement sufficient for the sins of His people—through all the centuries leading up to that Cross and in all the centuries leading away from it.

Beneath the cross of Jesus
I fain would take my stand.
The shadow of a mighty rock
Within a weary land;
A home within the wilderness,
A rest upon the way,
From the burning of the noontide heat,
And the burden of the day.

There lies beneath its shadow,
But on the farther side,
The darkness of an awful grave
That gapes both deep and wide:
And there between us stands the cross,
Two arms outstretched to save,
Like a watchman set to guard the way
From that eternal grave.

Upon that cross of Jesus,
Mine eye at times can see
The very dying form of One,
Who suffered there for me;
And from my stricken heart, with tears,
Two wonders I confess—
The wonders of His glorious love,
And my own worthlessness.
(Elizabeth Cecilia Clephane)

The wise and the foolish

The sun, shining down from a cloudless blue sky, was turning the cool, clear mountain water into ripples and eddies of gold as it swirled over the flat brownish green rocks; yet as the water poured smoothly over the edge of the waterfall it had the appearance of liquid glass, until it fell into the deep pool below in a cascade of crystal bubbles.

Almost mesmerised by the sight and sound of the falling water, I suddenly became aware of a pair of slim grey birds, with beautiful yellow breasts, flitting about on the rocks and watching me with some uncertainty. Both birds had their beaks full of insects and that could mean only one thing! I knew that if I sat still enough I would discover the destination of these grey wagtails. It was quite some minutes before they plucked up enough courage to approach their hidden nest, but at last they disappeared into a corner of the rock wall. When they had both discharged their cargo and flown away to forage for more, I carefully made my way over to the other side of the waterfall. Beneath a clump of ferns and behind a delicate screen of pink herb robert and yellow buttercups there was a neat little nest tucked into a crevice in the rock. As I gently put my finger on the nest immediately, as if released by a hidden spring, up popped three hopeful, gaping, yellow beaks. Very gently I touched the top of each downy little head, then backed away quietly to resume my patient vigil.

After two hours of watching those parent birds flying back and forth, back and forth, with never a moment's rest, I felt quite worn out. I wondered how they could keep it up, as presumably they did, from dawn until dusk (which, in mid-summer, would be at least 15 hours!)

On the fourth day after first discovering the nest, I arrived at the waterfall and saw one of the parent birds preening its feathers in the sun. "So they do stop sometimes," I thought. "Perhaps he is having a well-earned coffee break!" He flew away and, after waiting some minutes for the birds to return with food, I crossed the stream to peep into the nest. To my amazement it was empty! In my foolishness, I had rather hoped to see the fledglings leave the nest but those wise parent birds had encouraged them out of the nest, probably very early in the morning, supervising their first trial flights while there were no dangerous humans anywhere near to alarm or to interfere.

Where were they now? Probably they had wisely been taken upstream where fewer humans were likely to penetrate. I clambered over rocks and splashed through the water for about a quarter of a mile and, sure enough, there they were. I saw the parent birds and then, one after the other, three smaller birds (without the long tail feathers) flitting from tree to tree and even bouncing up into the sky twenty feet above my head. As I made my way down-stream one fledgling was sitting on a rock and I said to him, "Little do you know that I have actually touched your feathery head!" Words that I had read only that morning came, unbidden, into my mind again:

I know *and* am acquainted with all the birds of the mountains, and the wild animals of the field *are* Mine....

Psalm 50:11 (Amplified Version)

These wise parent birds had built their nest in a perfect situation, safely hidden from view, yet within reach of an endless

supply of cool flowing water and the necessary insect food. They had tirelessly tended their young when they were helpless; then, as soon as they could fend for themselves, they had removed them to a safe environment where they could develop their new powers unobserved and undisturbed. True, I saw a kestrel hovering up the valley, but that was a natural hazard and there were endless rocky crannies, with bracken and mountain-ash and silver birch trees to provide safe cover. I could not help drawing a sad comparison in my mind.

Wise parent birds—who had raised their young where there was an abundance of pure water and suitable food essential to their growth and development.

Foolish human parents—who, although endowed with greater intelligence, deliberately choose to raise their children on anything and everything but the bread and water of life found in the Word of God. Jesus said:

If any man thirst, let him come unto me, and drink.

John 7:37

But whosoever drinketh of the water that I shall give him shall never thirst; but the water that I shall give him shall be in him a well of water springing up into everlasting life.

John 4:14

Man shall not live by bread alone, but by every word that proceedeth out of the mouth of God.

Matthew 4:4

I am the bread of life: he that cometh to me shall never hunger; and he that believeth on me shall never thirst.

John 6:35

Foolish human parents—who will encourage their children in sport, picnics, outings, parties—but have no time or place for the things of God. Small wonder that their hearts are empty, their marriages break-up and their children often grow up spoiled and disobedient, an endless source of worry and disappointment.

For my people have committed two evils; they have forsaken me the fountain of living waters, *and* hewed them out cisterns, broken cisterns, that can hold no water.

Jeremiah 2:13

Suppose my little birds had decided to abandon their nest by the flowing stream and build it, instead, by a muddy stagnant pool where the water was gradually dwindling away. Their God-given bird sense would never lead them to be so foolish. Yet human parents, who should be so much wiser, do this very thing. They want nothing to do with God and turn with contempt from His Word, the only pure source of life and nourishment for the soul. They choose, instead, to bring up their children by the muddy, stagnant waters of worldly fashions, amusements and possessions.

I tried the broken cisterns, Lord,
But, ah, the waters failed!
E'en as I stooped to drink they fled,
And mocked me as I wailed.

Now none but Christ can satisfy,
None other Name for me;
There's love and life and lasting joy,
Lord Jesus, found in Thee.

(Author unknown)

Wise bird parents—carefully taking their young ones into a safe and suitable environment, free from unnecessary hazard, where they would learn how to fly, how and where to feed, how to preen their feathers, where to seek safety and shelter. By copying their parents, they could only learn what was good and useful for them—they would never learn any bad habits!

Foolish human parents—so often leading their children into harmful situations and by their own example, teaching them bad habits and evil language, either ignoring or forgetting the words of Solomon, wisest of kings, who said:

The fear of the LORD *is* the beginning of knowledge: *but* fools despise wisdom and instruction.

Proverbs 1:7

For wisdom *is* better than rubies; and all the things that may be desired are not to be compared to it.

Proverbs 8:11

I heard the voice of Jesus say,
'Behold, I freely give
The living water—thirsty one,
Stoop down, and drink, and live!'
I came to Jesus, and I drank
Of that life-giving stream;
My thirst was quenched, my soul revived,
And now I live in Him.

(Horatius Bonar)

As white as snow

One or two small flakes of snow, drifting gently down out of a grey sky—nothing to feel worried about. Gradually the flakes increase, falling thicker and faster, until there is a faint coating of white on the grass and the paths. Still they keep coming—thick, swirling, feathery flakes until everything in sight is covered with an inch of snow. All night long, through the darkness, the snowflakes fall unceasingly and in the morning, the sun rises upon a transformed world. From six to eight inches of snow balances precariously on the rose trellis and weighs down the branches of the fir trees, while the lawn is an expanse of white so pure and sparkling in the morning sun that it dazzles the eyes until they almost hurt.

With the snow there comes a strange, almost unearthly silence unknown at any other time. Up on the moor, the little pool is a world on its own, shut in by a curtain of falling snow that completely hides the mountains and valleys. There is no sound of calling birds, no sound of bleating sheep. The silence feels like the silence of eternity and there seems to be no one left in the world—no one but God.

Even on the edge of a busy city there is the same strange silence in the gardens. The traffic passing at the end of the road is muffled and, in the early winter twilight, 'phantom' electric trains glide quietly past, sending out unearthly pale blue flashes as they contact the snow piling on their rails. Only soft, feathery flakes—yet they can bring a great city to a standstill!

The freshly fallen untouched snow, dazzling white in the sunlight, gives us a picture of the indescribable holiness of God.

The snow as we ultimately see it, trodden underfoot and churned-up into a muddy, slushy mess at the side of the road gives us a picture, not of our sin (that would be bad enough) but of our own efforts at righteousness; our 'good works' which may seem reasonable in our eyes but which, in God's holy eyes, are as repulsive as the filthy slush is to us.

The sheep that look so delightfully white against a background of green grass, when seen against the newly fallen snow look wretched, dirty and bedraggled. Our lives, which seem highly commendable when compared with the lives of some of our neighbours or friends, look sadly repulsive when seen in the shining white light of God's holiness.

But we are all as an unclean *thing*, and all our righteousnesses *are* as filthy rags; *Isaiah 64:6*

If we know anything of our own hearts, we surely know that we can never hope to achieve a life that is pleasing to a God of such holiness. Suppose we only committed one sin each day, what would that amount to in an average lifetime? Suppose (if it were possible) that we did not commit another sin from this moment, what could we do about all our past sin? How could we possibly get rid of it? There is one way and only one. In His love and kindness, God offers us a 'robe of righteousness', the beautiful, holy life of the Lord Jesus Christ, pure as the driven snow, in place of our filthy rags.

Come now, and let us reason together, saith the LORD: though your sins be as scarlet, they shall be as white as snow; *Isaiah 1:18*

If we say that we have no sin, we deceive ourselves, and the truth is not in us. If we confess our sins, he is

faithful and just to forgive us *our* sins, and to cleanse us from all unrighteousness. *1 John 1:8-9*

Who would not gladly exchange the filthy, muddy slush for the dazzling whiteness of the untrodden snow? Who would not gladly exchange their own miserable efforts and good works for the gift of the holiness and righteousness that God offers to us in His Son? Who would not (oh! so thankfully) exchange their disobedience for His life of spotless and perfect obedience?

I will greatly rejoice in the LORD, my soul shall be joyful in my God; for he hath clothed me with the garments of salvation, he hath covered me with the robe of righteousness, ...

Isaiah 61:10

Jesus, Thy blood and righteousness
My beauty are, my glorious dress;
Midst flaming worlds, in these arrayed,
With joy shall I lift up my head.

Bold shall I stand in that great day,
For who aught to my charge shall lay?
Fully absolved through Thee I am,
From sin and fear, from guilt and shame.

This spotless robe the same appears
When ruined nature sinks in years;
No age can change its glorious hue,
The robe of Christ is ever new.

(Nicolaus Ludwig von Zinzendorf
tr. by John Wesley)

When God draws near

At the end of the lawn there is a gnarled old crab-apple tree, a very ordinary tree by day but quite enchanting when the moonlight is shining on its mass of white blossoms. One morning, after breakfast, I sat at the window watching two or three chaffinches flitting about in its branches, while a wren was trilling away in the hedge nearby. Suddenly, one of the chaffinches joyfully took off, flying toward the roof of the cottage. I heard a dull thud and there he lay, sprawled on the grass, with his wings and tail feathers spread-eagled around him. His eyes closed and his head fell limply forward but, after a second or two, he seemed to revive a little, though he still lay on the grass just as he had fallen.

I went into the garden and walked slowly up to him, near enough to stroke his little slate blue head and chestnut breast. He made no attempt to move but his eyes kept opening and closing. Not wishing to cause him unnecessary distress, I went back into the room and sat watching him through the window and, as I watched, I wondered.

What could that little bird know about me and the kind of life that I live? What could he understand, for example, about my driving a car down the motorway, or of my using a word processor? What could he understand about my using a telephone or a gas cooker or an electric iron, or of any of the multitude of things that I could do that were totally unknown to him? As C.S.Lewis would have said, there was no 'holding place' in his mind for any of my complex life. I was altogether 'other', an unknown giant whose presence only terrified him.

Little did he know how much I cared about him. Little did he know that, while he lay there on the grass for about twenty minutes, exposed to any passing cat, I was watching over him, ready to run to his protection should the need arise. Little did he know my delight and pleasure when I saw him suddenly perk up his head, shake his wings and fly away again, swift and happy and free.

How great a Being is the Living God, how altogether 'other'. What a fragment we know or understand of His ways or His thoughts, of the immensity of His power or the diversity of His working.

O the depth of the riches both of the wisdom and knowledge of God! how unsearchable *are* his judgments, and his ways past finding out!

For who hath known the mind of the Lord? or who hath been his counseller?

Or who hath first given to him, and it shall be recompensed unto him again?

For of him, and through him, and to him, *are* all things; to whom *be* glory for ever. Amen.

Romans 11:33-36

If God, in all His glory, were to draw near to us, we would be far more terrified of His presence than the chaffinch was of mine. Yet, although we are largely unaware of it, He is watching over us in all our varied circumstances, continually caring for us and ready to come to the aid of His children when they are most weak and helpless **....for He cares for you affectionately, and cares about you watchfully.**

1 Peter 5:7 (Amplified Version)

Most wonderful of all, in the Lord Jesus Christ, God can and does draw near to us, His presence no longer a terror but our greatest comfort and joy. Jesus Christ, who is God Himself, came to this earth in the form of a man, living, working and walking as Man among men. The aged apostle John wrote, with awe, of those early days in his own experience when he and the other disciples had walked and talked with the Lord of Glory, along the dusty roads of Galilee.

They had seen Him sitting tired, hungry and thirsty, upon the edge of the well in Samaria. They had looked into His face and seen Him weep over Jerusalem; they had heard the compassion in His voice when He addressed the multitudes and the authority with which He had rebuked the Pharisees. With shattered hopes they had seen Him 'crucified in weakness' and three days later, with almost unbelieving joy, they had seen Him after His resurrection and actually handled His risen and glorified body.

That which was from the beginning, which we have heard, which we have seen with our eyes, which we have looked upon, and our hands have handled, of the Word of life; ....That which we have seen and heard declare we unto you,

1 John 1:1 and 3

Yet when John was a prisoner on the Isle of Patmos and the Saviour appeared to him as the risen and ascended Lord of Glory, John—who had known Him so intimately; John—who had leaned upon His breast at the Last Supper; John 'fell at His feet as dead!' John's reaction shows how graciously the Lord had veiled His glory and majesty when He walked this earth as a Man.

It is a thing most wonderful,
Almost too wonderful to be,
That God's own Son should come from heaven,
And die to save a child like me.

And yet I know that it is true;
He came to this poor world below,
And wept and toiled and mourned and died,
Only because He loved us so.

I sometimes think about the cross,
And shut my eyes,and try to see
The cruel nails, and crown of thorns,
And Jesus crucified for me.

But even could I see Him die,
I could but see a little part
Of that great love which, like a fire,
Is always burning in His heart.

And yet I want to love Thee, Lord;
O light the flame within my heart,
And I will love Thee more and more
Until I see Thee as Thou art.
(William Walsham How)

Living velvet

Driving up a rutted country lane, trying to avoid the pot-holes, I suddenly became aware of a large expanse of pale blue on my left. A pale blue field—whoever heard of such a thing? It was not the rich, deep blue of a carpet of bluebells so I stopped to investigate. Previously the ground had been an orchard, but the old apple trees had been rooted out and the field newly sown with grass for sheep-grazing. Tender new green grass had sprung up quickly but so had thousands and thousands of tiny speedwell plants, so many that the general colour of the field really was pale blue instead of green.

Only a few days before I had been lying in the sun, studying the speedwell flowers that grew, not only in the lawn, but under the hedges and in the grass paths that bordered and intersected the kitchen garden. "Wretched weeds" my husband called them!

"Wretched weeds" no doubt they are to a gardener but oh! how exquisitely formed. At regular intervals up the fragile stem a tiny green rosette emerged, containing the beautiful three-petalled blue flowers. Further up the stem the delicate buds, tipped with palest blue, were ready to open as the lower flowers fell. The stalks on which these flowers and buds were hanging looked as fine as a hair, yet they were capable of drawing from the ground the moisture necessary to produce leaves, buds, flowers and, ultimately, minute seeds containing life. The sun (ninety-three million miles away) was causing three pencil-fine shadows to fall on the petals from the tiny stamens and pistil.

In that pale blue field there must have been millions of these delicate flowers. If a clever jeweller copied that speedwell, forming a dainty brooch with pale blue sapphires for the flowers and buds, people would probably pay a large sum of money for such a lovely ornament. Yet the real flower, fashioned by the hand of the Creator Himself, lies unheeded and unnoticed in the grass—a "wretched weed".

Consider the lilies of the field, how they grow; they toil not, neither do they spin; And yet I say unto you, That even Solomon in all his glory was not arrayed like one of these. *Matthew 6:28-29*

Why did our Lord say this? No doubt He had various reasons but surely one of them was that Solomon, most magnificent of kings, was only clothed in man-made silk and velvet, while the flowers of the field are clothed in living material. We touch the petals of a pansy and say, "They are just like velvet", but they are not. Velvet is a poor man-made imitation of the living velvet of the pansy or the wild heart's-ease. We touch the pale pink petals of a wild rose and say, "They are just like satin", but they are not. Satin is a poor, man-made imitation of the living satin of the rose petals. Yet these wonderful flowers, made by their Creator out of living velvet and living satin, only last for a day or two and then they are thrown upon the bonfire.

Wherefore, if God so clothe the grass of the field, which today is, and tomorrow is cast into the oven, *shall he* not much more *clothe* you, O ye of little faith? *Matthew 6:30*

Where does all this beauty originate? In a tiny brown speck of a seed, sometimes as small as a grain of pepper. Yet, contained within that speck is *life*—all the life necessary for root, leaves, flowers, dozens of buds and hundreds of similar seeds, every one containing that mysterious life that will reproduce identical flowers. Every flower and every seed is just one more of God's mighty miracles, just one more cause for worship and wonder on the part of His children.

Heaven above is softer blue,
Earth around is sweeter green;
Something lives in every hue
Christless eyes have never seen:
Birds with gladder songs o'erflow
Flowers with deeper beauties shine,
Since I know, as now I know,
I am His and He is mine.

His for ever, only His;
Who the Lord and me shall part?
Ah, with what a rest of bliss
Christ can fill the loving heart!
Heaven and earth may fade and flee,
First-born light in gloom decline,
But while God and I shall be,
I am His and He is mine.
(George Wade Robinson)

Roots and foundations

During the freak hurricane that passed over southern England in 1987 millions of trees were hurled to the ground. In many forests they went down like dominoes, the first tree falling against the next until a great swathe showed the path that the destroying wind had taken. Sevenoaks, in Kent, named for its seven mighty oak trees (originally planted in the reign of Charles I) found, with morning light, that only one of its famous trees was still standing. This amazing devastation was the combined effect of 100 mph winds following weeks of unusually heavy rainfall which had caused even the roots of well-matured trees to be holding loosely in the earth.

Most people take little notice of trees, regarding them as a natural background to the more interesting scenes of daily life, yet every tree is a daily revelation of God's almighty power. Barrels and barrels of water must be sent to the very tip of every tiniest twig on all the hundreds of branches, if the swelling buds are to unfold into new tender green leaves. Once formed, in order to keep them green and living, an endless supply of water must be sent up to these young leaves all through the gentle days of spring and the hot, burning weeks of summer. To move the necessary water to the tips of the branches, the roots of a mature tree have to exert a working pressure of 3,000 lbs per square foot, without taking into account the resistance of the wood in the tree trunk. Engineers will confirm that no pump that has ever been devised or designed by man could force that amount of water through the dense wooden trunk, yet God's power is doing this, every day, in all the millions and

millions and millions of trees throughout the world.

When a tree has been felled in our garden, I often stand looking at the sawn off trunk and run my hand over its surface and marvel—yes, *marvel* at the power of God which has sent the life-giving water, day after day, week after week, year after year, through this trunk which feels, to my touch, as solid and impenetrable as concrete.

O Lord, how manifold are thy works! In wisdom hast thou made them all: the earth is full of thy riches.

Psalm 104:24

There is something that is even more amazing. This mighty process takes place without a sound. Walk through an avenue of ancient beech trees with their vast silver-grey trunks and their myriads of branches reaching upward to the sky and what do you hear? On a still autumn day there is nothing but the faint stirring of a breeze in the branches; the gentle falling to the ground of curling, bronze coloured leaves; the rustling of your own feet as you walk on the carpet of already fallen leaves; perhaps the distant murmur of a woodland stream, but not a sound to indicate the tremendous force that is endlessly pumping life up, up, up through those solid tree trunks. Imagine the continual noise and turmoil if man-made pumps were working in every tree! The din would be unbearable. Who but the Almighty could work with such power and such silence?

Many of the great trees that fell in the hurricane, some being several hundred years old, were overturned because their roots were spreading sideways beneath the surface rather than down into the depth of the earth.

The Lord Jesus Christ told a parable, not of a tree, but of a house that had weak foundations which were the cause of its downfall when great winds and storms came against it.

Therefore whosoever heareth these sayings of mine, and doeth them, I will liken him unto a wise man, which built his house upon a rock: And the rain descended, and the floods came, and the winds blew, and beat upon that house; and it fell not: for it was founded upon a rock. And every one that heareth these sayings of mine, and doeth them not, shall be likened unto a foolish man, which built his house upon the sand: And the rain descended, and the floods came, and the winds blew, and beat upon that house; and it fell: and great was the fall of it.

Matthew 7:24-27

When gale-force winds are sweeping across the moor, hurling themselves against the walls of the cottage and lashing the rain against the windows, how comforting it is to lie snugly in bed, knowing that there are solid foundations that can withstand all the raging of the storm. This is true of spiritual storms also. There are times when the Lord allows the enemy of our souls to come against His children and his attack feels as pitiless and merciless as a storm driving against the wall. Our only comfort then is to know that the foundation of our faith is not in our feelings but in the solid promises of our Lord, that He will hold us and be our refuge and strength in these times of great stress.

For thou hast been a strength to the poor, a strength to the needy in his distress, a refuge from the storm, a shadow from the heat, when the blast of the terrible ones *is* as a storm *against* the wall. *Isaiah 25:4*

Whether we speak of trees or of houses, the principle is the same. Only deep roots and strong foundations can withstand the fierce and terrible storms of life. Only faith and belief that is rooted deeply in the words and teachings of the Lord Jesus Christ will hold us steady in the fearful storms of life and in the solemn hour of death.

How firm a foundation, ye saints of the Lord,
Is laid for your faith in His excellent Word!
What more can He say than to you He has said—
You, who unto Jesus for refuge have fled?

Fear not, I am with thee, O be not dismayed!
I, I am thy God, and will still give thee aid:
I'll strengthen thee, help thee, and cause thee to stand,
Upheld by My righteous, omnipotent hand.

When through the deep waters I cause thee to go,
The rivers of woe shall not thee overflow;
For I will be with thee, thy troubles to bless,
And sanctify to thee thy deepest distress.

When through fiery trials thy pathway shall lie,
My grace all-sufficient shall be thy supply;
The flame shall not hurt thee; I only design
Thy dross to consume, and thy gold to refine.

The soul that on Jesus has leaned for repose
I will not, I will not desert to its foes;
That soul, though all hell should endeavour to shake,
I'll never, no never, no never forsake!

('K'—in Rippon's Selection)

Cover my defenceless head

It is said that Charles Wesley was sitting, one day, by a large open window in the country house where his Mother was born, when a violent storm arose. He continued to sit at the window, watching the play of the lightning and listening to the crashing thunder. Suddenly, at the height of the storm, a terrified sparrow came hurtling through the window and took refuge inside Wesley's coat where it clung, trembling, all the time the storm lasted. When at last the storm had lessened, Wesley gently withdrew the little bird from his waistcoat and set it free to fly swiftly out of the window.

Some people think that this was the inspiration of Charles Wesley's hymn, one of the loveliest in our language:

Jesu, Lover of my soul,
Let me to Thy bosom fly,
While the nearer waters roll,
While the tempest still is high:
Hide me, O my Saviour, hide,
Till the storm of life be past;
Safe into the haven guide;
O receive my soul at last!

It is not certain, however, whether that is a true story or merely a beautiful illustration of this well-loved hymn. What is certainly known is that, during the last century, another fearful and violent storm was raging at sea and about twenty small boats were struggling to reach land. The captain of one of the boats was a Christian and at last, when all hope had been abandoned, he gathered the crew and the passengers together, and they prayed and sang Wesley's hymn. Of all those twenty boats, *that one alone survived in the terrible Lossiemouth disaster.*

The thought of a bird, hiding from danger, is often used in the Bible to describe the Lord's care and protection of His people in times of great distress. The psalmist had this in mind when he cried: **Yea, in the shadow of thy wings will I make my refuge, until *these* calamities be overpast.** *Psalm 57:1*

He shall cover thee with his feathers, and under his wings shalt thou trust: *Psalm 91:4*

The mother hen, pecking here and there, struts jerkily across the barnyard floor while her yellow chicks, scattered far and wide, are eagerly exploring all the nooks and crannies. Suddenly, the deadly shadow of a bird of prey hovers above them. Immediately, the old hen gives her warning call and little fluffy bundles come scurrying from all directions to hide under her outstretched wings. The hen will face the enemy, so that the attack will fall upon her and not upon the chicks who are safely hidden from all danger beneath her sheltering wings.

My God, how excellent Thy grace,
Whence all our hope and comfort springs!
The sons of Adam, in distress
Fly to the shadow of Thy wings .
(Isaac Watts)

Our Lord Himself used this lovely picture as He rode into Jerusalem. He wept as He looked down upon the city of God where He knew that, in a few days, He would be rejected, scourged and crucified, but it was not for Himself that He wept.

O Jerusalem, Jerusalem, *thou* that killest the prophets and stonest them which are sent unto thee, how often

would I have gathered thy children together, even as a hen gathereth her chickens under *her* wings, and ye would not! *Matthew 23:37*

Other refuge have I none;
Hangs my helpless soul on Thee;
Leave, ah! leave me not alone,
Still support and comfort me:
All my trust on Thee is stayed,
All my help from Thee I bring;
Cover my defenceless head
With the shadow of Thy wing.

Thou, O Christ, art all I want;
More than all in Thee I find;
Raise the fallen, cheer the faint,
Heal the sick, and lead the blind:
Just and holy is Thy name,
I am all unrighteousness;
False and full of sin I am,
Thou art full of truth and grace.

Plenteous grace with Thee is found,
Grace to cover all my sin;
Let the healing streams abound,
Make and keep me pure within:
Thou of life the fountain art,
Freely let me take of Thee;
Spring Thou up within my heart,
Rise to all eternity.

(Charles Wesley)

Green leaf in drought

Week after week of brilliant blue skies and blazing sunshine. How we revelled in it—and how we paid for it! Forbidden to use either hose or sprinkler, we watched our plants begin to wither and the grass become scorched and brown. Dedicated gardeners were reduced to carrying out bowls and buckets of washing-up water to throw on their thirsty flowers.

There is a small, natural spring flowing from inside the hill at the back of our garden and we tried, with much difficulty and little success, to syphon some of its surplus water across the lawn to the various flower beds. As the weeks went by and the drought continued, with no sign of the longed-for rain, we began to transplant some of our favourite plants and roots to the bed where the spring came out of the hillside. Here, in the moist earth, pink, white, purple and pale mauve phlox flourished, in company with some roses that were there already, while marigolds and montbretia added bright splashes of orange and yellow amongst the green ferns. The rest of the garden was just a burnt-up wilderness.

When visitors came to the garden they would walk round the side of the house and then stop dead with amazement, exclaiming, "How do you have this riot of flowers and colour and fresh green? Everyone else's garden is a total write-off!" Then we would explain about the hidden source of water and show them the never-ending spring, pouring out its one pint of water in just under one minute. In the hottest, driest time of that drought the spring never failed, steadily trickling through—never more, never less—giving life to the plants and birds and pleasure to the garden's visitors and owners.

Blessed *is* the man that walketh not in the counsel of the ungodly, nor standeth in the way of sinners, nor sitteth in the seat of the scornful. But his delight *is* in the law of the LORD; and in his law doth he meditate day and night. And he shall be like a tree planted by the rivers of water, that bringeth forth his fruit in his season; his leaf also shall not wither; and whatsoever he doeth shall prosper.

Psalm 1:1-3

What do we know of green leaves in drought? In times of sickness and trouble, in adversity of all kinds, are our 'leaves' green and healthy because we are feeding on the Word of God and drinking from the water of life, or are they dry and shrivelled and our 'flowers' sickly and drooping?

Blessed *is* the man that trusteth in the LORD, and whose hope the LORD is. For he shall be as a tree planted by the waters, and *that* spreadeth out her roots by the river, and shall not see when heat cometh, but her leaf shall be green; and shall not be careful in the year of drought, neither shall cease from yielding fruit. *Jeremiah 17:7-8*

There is a stream that has its source somewhere in the heart of the Brecon Beacons. When almost all the waterfalls had disappeared and every reservoir had reached a record 'low', this stream continued, all through the drought, to pour forth a steady flow of life-giving water. On any of those hot, burning days it was possible to sit on the grassy bank near the waterfall and bathe one's feet in the cold, refreshing water flowing from the hidden source that never, never failed.

(Jesus said) **If any man thirst, let him come unto me, and drink. He that believeth on me, as the scripture hath said, out of his belly shall flow rivers of living water.**

John 7:37-38

Like a river glorious
Is God's perfect peace,
Over all victorious
In its bright increase;
Perfect, yet it floweth
Fuller every day;
Perfect, yet it groweth
Deeper all the way.

Hidden in the hollow
Of His blessèd hand,
Never foe can follow,
Never traitor stand;
Not a surge of worry,
Not a shade of care,
Not a blast of hurry
Touch the spirit there.

Every joy or trial
Falleth from above,
Traced upon our dial
By the Sun of Love:
We may trust Him fully
All for us to do;
They who trust Him wholly
Find Him wholly true.

Stayed upon Jehovah,
Hearts are fully blest;
Finding, as He promised,
Perfect peace and rest.

(Frances Ridley Havergal)

For fruit or fire

Apple-blossom—tight coral pink buds; paler pink buds beginning to unfold; pink and white flowers wide open to the sun, all against a background of pale grey satin branches and blue sky. Beneath the trees, clusters of delicate yellow primroses were opening to the warm spring sunshine, with even an occasional cowslip here and there. A long-tailed tit flitted through the wild rhododendron and, further down the garden, a pair of bullfinches chased each other in and out of the bushes. I picked one or two twigs of apple blossom to put in a vase in my kitchen so that I could enjoy them while I was working.

A couple of days later I went again to the orchard to look at the apple-blossom but, meantime, there had been cold north winds and an unexpected hailstorm. Many of the flowers were bruised and battered, the petals turning brown at the edges, nothing like the perfect blooms that I had admired previously. I thought of the blossoms in my kitchen, still beautiful, protected and unharmed by wind or hail. They had escaped the storm, *but they would never bear any fruit.* The blossoms on the trees in the orchard, bruised and beaten though they were by the harsh weather, would yet fulfil God's purpose for them and produce beautiful apples in the autumn.

The most fruitful lives are always those that have come through storm and buffeting, not those that have been sheltered and protected. God's servant Job probably suffered more than any other mortal man. First he lost his family and his immense wealth; then, when he was stricken with a loathsome disease

that made his days a living death, his wife advised him to 'curse God and die' while his well-meaning friends did their utmost to rob him of his godly reputation. Yet his example of unswerving confidence in the faithfulness of God, in the midst of his appalling suffering, has been a source of blessing and encouragement to God's people through all the centuries.

Though he slay me, yet will I trust in him. *Job 13:15*

But he knoweth the way that I take: *when* he hath tried me, I shall come forth as gold. *Job 23:10*

Joseph, betrayed by his brothers and sold as a slave into Egypt; wrongfully accused by an evil woman and thrown into prison; forgotten for two years by the butler who had promised to speak on his behalf—Joseph knew what cruel suffering meant, yet he was able ultimately to say:

For God hath caused me to be fruitful in the land of my affliction. *Genesis 41:52*

Now no chastening for the present seemeth to be joyous, but grievous: nevertheless afterward it yieldeth the peaceable fruit of righteousness unto them which are exercised thereby. *Hebrews 12:11*

Now, the pruning, sharp, unsparing,
Scattered blossom, bleeding shoot:
Afterward, the plenteous bearing
Of the Master's pleasant fruit.

Now, the spirit conflict riven,
Wounded heart, unequal strife;
Afterward, the triumph given,
And the victor's crown of life.

Now, the training, strange and lowly,
Unexplained and tedious now;
Afterward, the service holy,
And the Master's 'Enter thou'.
(Frances Ridley Havergal)

Honeysuckle—one year it grew in such profusion that there was literally a cascade of honeysuckle; hundreds of sweet-scented creamy blossoms, tinged with pink, falling down the side of the house, a joy to behold and a delight to give away to friends. The perfume, as it rose in the evening sunshine up to the bedroom window, was almost intoxicating.

Why, then, was I to be found next year, sawing through the thick stems, pulling the branches away from the wall and hurriedly dragging the whole enormous bundle down the garden to the the bonfire? There was a sad and valid reason. The honeysuckle was no longer a joy and delight. It was diseased, dripping and sticky with greenfly, so that the flowers could not even begin to open. That which should have been a joy and a pleasure had become hideous, an eyesore in the garden and only fit for burning.

God made Adam and Eve for His own pleasure and delight and for their blessing, intending that He and they should walk together in the beautiful world He had made, delighting in each other's company.

Thou art worthy, O Lord, to receive glory and honour and power: for thou hast created all things, and for thy pleasure they are and were created. *Revelation 4:11*

But, by one act of deliberate disobedience, they became defiled and hideous in His sight. All men and women (because they are descended from Adam and Eve) are spoiled and diseased by sin so that the holy God can no longer take any pleasure in them. Yet, although we are now only fit for destruction, in His great love and mercy He has made a way, through the life and atoning death of the Lord Jesus Christ, for us to be delivered from this terrible disease of sin and made, once again, objects of delight to Him.

God made me for Himself, to serve Him here,
With love's pure service and in filial fear;
To show His praise, for Him to labour now;
Then see His glory where the angels bow.

All needful grace was mine through His dear Son,
Whose life and death my full salvation won;
The grace that would have strengthened me, and taught;
Grace that would crown me when my work was wrought.

And I, poor sinner, cast it all away;
Lived for the toil or pleasure of each day;
As if no Christ had shed His precious blood,
As if I owed no homage to my God.

O Holy Spirit, with Thy fire divine,
Melt into tears this thankless heart of mine;
Teach me to love what once I seemed to hate,
And live to God before it be too late.

(Sir Henry Williams Baker)

The Bible, which so often likens sin to the loathsome disease of leprosy, shows in two beautiful verses the simplicity with which a sinful soul, realising its dreadful condition, can come to the Lord for healing.

And, behold, there came a leper and worshipped him, saying, Lord, if thou wilt, thou canst make me clean. And Jesus put forth *his* hand, and touched him, saying, I will; be thou clean. And immediately his leprosy was cleansed.

Matthew 8:2-3

Jesus, I will trust Thee,
Trust Thee with my soul;
Guilty, lost, and helpless,
Thou canst make me whole:
There is none in heaven
Or on earth like Thee:
Thou hast died for sinners—
Therefore, Lord, for me.

Jesus, I must trust Thee,
Pondering Thy ways,
Full of love and mercy
All Thine earthly days:
Sinners gathered round Thee,
Lepers sought Thy face;
None too vile or loathsome
For a Saviour's grace.

Jesus, I can trust Thee,
Trust Thy written Word,
Though Thy voice of pity
I have never heard:
When Thy Spirit teacheth,
To my taste how sweet!
Only may I hearken,
Sitting at Thy feet.

Jesus, I do trust Thee,
Trust without a doubt;
Whosoever cometh
Thou wilt not cast out;
Faithful is Thy promise,
Precious is Thy blood:
These my soul's salvation,
Thou my Saviour God!

(Mary Jane Walker)

If God knows—why must I pray?

There is a robin in my garden who feeds from my hand. When I open my bedroom window, a little brown and rust-coloured bird swoops off the swings at the end of the lawn, flies over to the lilac bushes and then up to the window-sill for his morning crumbs. Sometimes I have felt the grip of his tiny claws as he clings to my finger, reaching for the crumbs in the palm of my hand.

One spring day, when I was tired of sweeping up piles of dead leaves and pine-needles for the bonfire, I climbed the primrose bank and sat down to rest on an old silver birch log. As I sat gazing up into the bare branches of the beech tree—black lace traced against blue sky—out of the corner of my eye I saw a flutter of wings. I knew that my robin had followed me, as he always did, hoping for some biscuit crumbs. Still sitting in the same position, I pretended that I had not seen him. He fluttered and flirted his tail, hopping nearer and nearer, until he was within a few inches. Still I pretended I had not seen him. At last, in desperation, he began to twitter and sing, plainly saying, "Can't you see me? Where are my crumbs? Surely there is something in your pocket for me?"

Why did I pretend not to see him? Why did I not give him the crumbs at once? Why, when I had deliberately brought them for him? *Because I wanted him to ask for them.* I wanted to hear his sweet, plaintive song and so I kept him waiting until, at last, he asked me for what he wanted.

Why does God seem, at times, not to hear? Why, when His loving heart has devised blessings and benefits for us which He knows we need and which He longs to give—why does He continue to withold them? For the same reason that I withheld crumbs from my robin. God delights to be asked. He, also, loves to hear the voice of His children asking Him for the very things He is intending to bestow upon them.

Prayer was appointed to convey
The blessings God designs to give;
Long as they live should Christians pray,
For only while they pray, they live.
(Joseph Hart)

Prayer is not, as we often sadly give the impression, the way to 'get things' from God, although we do ask and we do receive. Prayer is our drawing near to God and God drawing near to us, a fellowship between those who delight in each other. How incredible that we should be able to give God pleasure! Yet, because He is our Father, our dearest Friend, the Lover of our soul, He has said that the prayer of the upright is His delight.

Trust in him at all times; ye people, pour out your heart before him: God is a refuge for us. *Psalm 62:8*

Prayer is the burden of a sigh,
The falling of a tear,
The upward glancing of an eye
When none but God is near.

Prayer is the simplest form of speech,
That infant lips can try;
Prayer, the sublimest strains that reach
The Majesty on high.

Prayer is the contrite sinner's voice,
Returning from his ways;
While angels in their songs rejoice,
And cry, 'Behold, he prays!'

Prayer is the Christian's vital breath,
The Christian's native air,
His watchword at the gates of death;
He enters heaven with prayer.
(James Montgomery)

One day, an old farm worker was sitting under the hedge by the roadside, eating his frugal lunch. He held out some crumbs to a little robin who, too afraid to draw near, was watching him with bright-eyed interest. "Come to me; O come to me," coaxed the old man, "You don't know what good things I have for you." As he said those words, he suddenly realised that this was what God was saying to him. For some long time he had wanted to know how to come to God and he seemed to hear Him saying the very same words to him, "Come to Me; O come to Me. You don't know what good things I have for you." In this gracious way God ministered to the old man, showing him how simply he could come to the Lord and receive the blessings and joys of salvation that He was waiting to give him.

Just as I am, without one plea
But that Thy blood was shed for me,
And that Thou bidd'st me come to Thee,
O Lamb of God, I come.

Just as I am, and waiting not
To rid my soul of one dark blot,
To Thee, whose blood can cleanse each spot,
O Lamb of God, I come.

Just as I am, though tossed about
With many a conflict, many a doubt,
Fightings and fears within, without,
O Lamb of God, I come.

Just as I am, poor, wretched, blind:
Sight, riches, healing of the mind,
Yea, all I need, in Thee to find,
O Lamb of God, I come.

Just as I am, Thou wilt receive,
Wilt welcome, pardon, cleanse, relieve;
Because Thy promise I believe,
O Lamb of God, I come.

Just as I am—Thy love unknown
Has broken every barrier down—
Now to be Thine, yea, Thine alone,
O Lamb of God, I come.

Just as I am, of that free love
The breadth, length, depth, and height to prove.
Here for a season, then above,
O Lamb of God, I come.
(Charlotte Elliott)

Watching for the morning

Watching for the morning can be a delight. If the body is fit, but the mind awake and restless, it can be sheer joy to stand at the open window feeling the coolness of the morning air; to hear the wind sighing in the pine trees; to see a faint glimmer of light in the east and, in the strange half-light, to catch the gleaming white wings of the seagulls as they fly inland, skimming low over the dark, swiftly flowing river; then, at last, to see the cloud breaking into fleecy patches as the sun lights up the craggy outcrops of rock, and the golden tops of beech or silver birch among the banks of dark green fir trees. This kind of 'watching for the morning' is delightful, when no words are needed because:

Praise is silent for thee, O God, *Psalm 65:1 (margin)*

Watching for the morning can be a weary burden to those who have lain awake in pain and sleeplessness, waiting for the long, tedious hours of the night to pass. "One o'clock; two o'clock; three o'clock; will the night never end?" Oh! the relief to hear the first cars passing along the road or the first tentative notes of the robin, indicating that the world is coming alive again, that the long vigil is over. Oh! the relief to hear movements in the ward kitchen, the rattling of tea cups, the day-staff taking over from the night-staff. The long, weary night is ended and the morning has come at last!

I wait for the LORD, my soul doth wait, and in his word do I hope. My soul *waiteth* for the LORD more than they that watch for the morning: *I say, more than* they that watch for the morning. *Psalm 130:5-6*

Both these experiences—delightful expectancy and wearying vigil—blend together for the Christian as he waits and watches for the coming of his Lord. Sometimes he feels the weariness of the way; life is a burden, a dreary plodding through an ever darkening and ever worsening world, a continual 'night of doubt and sorrow'. It seems as though it will never end, that the dawn of eternity will never come.

Through the night of doubt and sorrow,
Onward goes the pilgrim band,
Singing songs of expectation,
Marching to the promised land.

One the light of God's own presence,
O'er His ransomed people shed,
Chasing far the gloom and terror
Brightening all the path we tread.
(Bernhardt Severin Ingemann)

At other times his spirit is cheered and quickened at the thought of his soon coming Lord and he comforts his heart with those gracious words:

Let not your heart be troubled: ye believe in God, believe also in me. In my Father's house are many mansions: if *it were* not *so*, I would have told you. I go to prepare a place for you. And if I go and prepare a place for you, I will come again, and receive you unto myself; that where I am, there ye may be also.

John 14:1-3

Then his spirit strains forward and, with the eye of faith, he gazes expectantly through the murky darkness of this world toward that great day when the night of doubt and sorrow will have ended and the Day Star shall have risen at last; when eternal glory will have dawned upon his soul and he will be forever in that dear Presence.

There's a light upon the mountains, and the day is at the spring,
When our eyes shall see the beauty and the glory of the King;
Weary was our heart with waiting, and the night-watch seemed so long,
But His triumph-day is breaking, and we hail it with a song.

There's a hush of expectation, and a quiet in the air:
And the breath of God is moving in the fervent breath of prayer;
For the suffering, dying Jesus is the Christ upon the throne,
And the travail of our spirits is the travail of His own.

Hark! we hear a distant music, and it comes with fuller swell;
'Tis the triumph song of Jesus, of our King Emmanuel;
Zion, go ye forth to meet Him: and my soul, be swift to bring
All thy sweetest and thy dearest for the triumph of the King!
(Henry Burton)

How I 'accidentally' climbed the Brecon Beacons

Nothing was further from my thoughts on that lovely June morning. Telling my husband that I would not be long, I drove up the valley to spend an hour by my favourite stream, which runs down from the Beacons into the Beacons Reservoir. The wind was too cool for me to sit by the waterfall so I decided to walk further upstream than I had been before, perhaps even to find its source.

It was a leisurely walk, because I kept stopping to watch a pair of dippers and several slender grey wagtails. At one point I came up so quietly behind a sheep grazing at the water's edge that, as I passed her, she gave a violent start of surprise and fell side-ways into the stream. "That will be jolly," I thought, "if I have to heave a sodden-wet sheep out the water!" Fortunately she rolled over the stones until she was on her feet and then hastily scrambled up the further bank, with her bewildered lamb following. The commotion this made, and my apology to the sheep, disturbed a grey heron and sent him flapping over the hill with his slow, slow wing beat.

Having by this time travelled about a mile upstream I decided to make tracks for home, knowing that it would take some hard walking to retrace my way down again. It was then that I had my first bright idea. If I climbed the steep bank on my right, I would be able to see how much further the stream extended. Then I could walk back, much more easily and quickly, down the official mountain path that leads to and from Corn

Du and Pen-y-Fan (pronounced *Corn Dee* and *Pen-a-Van*). I struggled with some difficulty up about fifty feet or so of very rough grassland—only to discover that the stream, of course, had diverged and the path I had expected to find at the top of the bank was at least three-quarters of a mile away! Well, there was no point in going back. It would still be easier to go home down the path, so I toiled wearily on and on, over rushes and bog and tussocks of grass. The Beacons were about a mile away on my left and it was then that I had my second bright idea. Quite by accident, I was nearer than I had ever been to the top of the Beacons. Should I go down the path, when I finally reached it, or should I go up? It seemed such a pity to waste all my effort and it was unlikely that I would ever be this near again! I made the momentous decision—*I would go up!*

I climbed on and on, and up and up, pausing occasionally to regain my breath and look back over the way I had so far come. Only then did I realise that I had climbed the Beacons by a much harder route than necessary. If only I had come by the official path how much easier it would have been! Would I ever finally arrive at the top? Coming without intention, I had no binoculars with me, only a pair of antique mother-of-pearl glasses which, being very small, I always kept in my pocket for bird-watching. As I met dedicated climbers striding down the path with their maps and binoculars, I carefully kept my glasses hidden under the mac which I was carrying!

At last I reached the first peak, Corn Du, and sat gazing at fold upon fold of misty blue mountains. I saw the deep blue-black tarn that I had heard about from other climbers and I studied the 'back' of the Beacons which, until now, I had only seen on photographs. It was very wonderful but the greatest thrill of all was that *I was there!* I could hardly believe it to be true. I was the one who had never evinced any desire to climb the Beacons. If other people wanted to climb mountains they were welcome to do so, but I was quite happy meandering along the stream watching my birds. Yet here I was, at the very top.

I could see down into the valley where I had wandered so aimlessly. I could see the rough mountainside over which I had toiled so painfully. I could see the long stretch of path up which I had climbed so endlessly, wondering if I would ever really reach the top.

There is nothing original in likening the Christian life to a mountain climb, but all who enjoy the glories of heaven will be full of praise to God for the grace that has brought them there. They will look back over the whole journey, as I did over my climb, remembering the time when they had no desire after the things of God. If other people believed all that stuff about God, heaven and hell—well, let them. They were going to follow their own paths and plans and had no intention of letting God, or anyone else, interfere. But there came a day when they were drawn off their own path and forced upward. God has many ways of doing this. For our own sakes He would lead us by the easier official path, but we usually decide to do it the hard way (as I did) so that He has to use circumstances of all kinds to draw us upward on to the only path. For there is only one way to reach God and that is by repentance, and faith in the true and living Way, the Lord Jesus Christ Himself.

I am the way, the truth, and the life: no man cometh unto the Father, but by me. *John 14:6*

Having said that, many and varied are the ways of coming to Christ, some of them difficult and painful. What does that matter as long as we do come to Him and, following Him, arrive at last 'at the top', in heaven itself, there to behold and to enjoy things unknown and undreamed of before?

He and I, in that bright Glory,
One deep joy shall share;
Mine, to be forever with Him;
His, that I am there. (Gerhard Tersteegen)

John Bunyan, John Newton and George Müller, to name but three, wandered in the sin, darkness and degradation of their own way until God, in His mercy and by His Spirit, compelled them toward the one true Way. Little did they dream in their earlier days, that they would ever reach Heaven's glory. What grace and mercy that they, of all people, should be there! Yet even the greatest and godliest servants of the Lord will marvel at the grace of God that has brought them into His Presence. They will look back over the way they have travelled, at the things they have suffered but, most of all, at the merciful leadings of God. Remembering their sin and their waywardness, each one will exclaim "Why, O Lord, such love to me?'

From heavenly Jerusalem's towers,
The path through the desert they trace;
And every affliction they suffered
Redounds to the glory of grace;
Their look they cast back on the tempests,
On fears, on grim death and the grave,
Rejoicing that now they're in safety,
Through Him that is mighty to save.

And we, from the wilds of the desert,
Shall flee to the land of the blest;
Life's tears shall be changed to rejoicing,
Its labours and toil into rest.
There we shall find refuge eternal,
From sin, from affliction, from pain,
And in the sweet love of the Saviour,
A joy without end shall attain.
(David Charles—
translated by Lewis Edwards)

Angels holy,
High and lowly,
Sing the praises of the Lord!
Earth and sky, all living nature,
Man, the stamp of thy Creator,
Praise ye, praise ye, God the Lord!

Sun and moon bright,
Night and noon-light,
Starry temples azure-floored.
Cloud and rain, and wild winds' madness,
Sons of God that shout for gladness,
Praise ye, praise ye, God the Lord!

Ocean hoary,
Tell His glory,
Cliffs, where tumbling seas have roared,
Pulse of waters, blithely beating,
Wave advancing, wave retreating,
Praise ye, praise ye, God the Lord!

Rock and high land,
Wood and island,
Crag, where eagle's pride hath soared;
Mighty mountains, purple-breasted,
Peaks cloud-cleaving, snowy-crested,
Praise ye, praise ye, God the Lord!

Rolling river,
Praise Him ever,
From the mountain's deep vein poured;
Silver fountains, clearly gushing,
Troubled torrent, madly rushing,
Praise ye, praise ye, God the Lord!

Praise Him ever,
Bounteous Giver!
Praise Him, Father, Friend, and Lord!
Each glad soul its free course winging,
Each glad voice its free song singing,
Praise the great and mighty Lord!
(J.S.Blackie)

Now unto him that is able to keep you from falling, and to present *you* faultless before the presence of his glory with exceeding joy, To the only wise God our Saviour, *be* glory and majesty, dominion and power, both now and ever. Amen. *Jude :24-25*